Autobiography and Selected Essays

Thomas Henry Huxley

Contents

AUTOBIOGRAPHY AND SELECTED ESSAYS

BY

Thomas Henry Huxley

PREFACE

THE purpose of the following selections is to present to students of English a few of Huxley's representative es-says. Some of these selections are complete; others are extracts. In the latter case, however, they are not extracts in the sense of being incomplete wholes, for each selection given will be found to have, in Aristotle's phrase, "a beginning, a middle, and an end." That they are complete in themselves, although only parts of whole essays, is due to the fact that Huxley, in order to make succeeding material clear, often prepares the way with a long and careful definition. Such is the nature of the extract *A Liberal Education,* in reality a definition to make distinct and forcible his ideas on the shortcomings of English schools. Such a definition, also, is *The Method of Scientific Investigation.*

The footnotes are those of the author. Other notes on the text have been included for the benefit of schools in-adequately equipped with reference books. It is hoped, however, that, the notes may be found not to be so numerous as to prevent the training of the student in a self-reliant and scholarly use of dictionaries and reference books; it is hoped, also, that they may serve to stimulate him to trace out for himself more completely any subject connected with the text in which he may feel a peculiar interest. It should be recognized that notes are of value only as they develop power to read intelligently. If unintelligently relied upon, they may even foster indifference and lazy mental habits.

I wish to express my obligation to Miss Flora Bridges, whose careful reading of the manuscript has been most helpful, and to Professor Clara F. Stevens, the head of the English Department at Mount Holyoke College, whose very . practical aid made this volume possible.

INTRODUCTION

I
THE LIFE OF HUXLEY

OF Huxley's life and of the forces which moulded his thought, the *Autobiography* gives some account; hut many facts which are significant are slighted, and necessarily the later events of his life are omitted. To supplement the story as given by him is the purpose of this sketch. The facts for this account are gathered entirely from the *Life and Letters of Thomas Henry Huxley*, by his son. For a real acquaintance with Huxley, the student should consult this source for himself; he will count the reading of the *Life and Letters* among the rare pleasures which have come to him through books.

Thomas Henry Huxley was born on May 4, 1825. His autobiography gives a full account of his parents, his early boyhood, and his education. Of formal education, Huxley had little; but he had the richer schooling which nature and life give an eager mind. He read widely; he talked often with older people; he was always investigating the why of things. He kept a journal in which he noted thoughts gathered from books, and ideas on the causes of certain phenomena. In this journal he frequently wrote what he had done and had set himself to do in the way of increasing his knowledge. Self-conducted, also, was his later education at the Charing Cross Hospital. Here, like Stevenson in his university days, Huxley seemed to be idle, but in reality, he was always busy on his own private end. So constantly did he work over the microscope that the window at which he sat came to be dubbed by his fellow students " The Sign of the Head and Microscope." Moreover, in his regular courses at Charing Cross, he seems to have done work sufficiently notable to be recognized by several prizes and a gold medal.

Of his life after the completion of his medical coarse, of his search for work, of his appointment as assistant surgeon on hoard the Rattlesnake, and of his searoh scientific work daring the four years' cruise, for work. Huxley gives a vivid description in the autobiography. As a result of his investigations on this voyage, he published various essays which quickly secured for him a position in the scientific world as a naturalist of the first rank. A testimony of the value of this work was his election to membership in the Royal Society.

Although Huxley had now, at the age of twenty-six, won distinction in science, he soon discovered that it was not so easy to earn bread thereby. Nevertheless, to earn a living was most important if he were to accomplish the two objects which he had in view. He wished, in the first place, to marry Miss Henrietta Heathorn of Sydney, to whom he had become engaged when on the cruise with the Rattlesnake; his second object was to follow science as a profession. The struggle to find something connected with science which would pay was long and bitter; and only a resolute determination to win kept Huxley from abandoning it altogether. Uniform ill-luck met him every where. He has told in his autobiography of his troubles with the Admiralty in the endeavor to get his papers published, and of his failure there. He applied for a position to teach science in Toronto; being unsuccessful in this attempt, he applied successively for various professorships in the United Kingdom, and in this he was likewise unsuccessful. Some of his friends urged him to hold out, but others thought the fight an unequal one, and advised him to emigrate to Australia. He himself was tempted to practice medicine in Sydney; but to give up his purpose seemed to him like cowardice. On the other hand, to prolong the struggle indefinitely when he might quickly earn a living in other ways seemed like selfishness and an injustice to the woman to whom he had been for a long time engaged. Miss Heathorn, however, upheld him in his determination to pursue science; and his sister also, he writes, cheered him by her advice and encouragement to persist in the struggle. Something of the man's heroic temper may be gathered from a letter which he wrote to Miss Heathorn when his affairs were darkest. "However painful our separation may be," he says, " the spectacle of a man who had given up the cherished purpose of his life . . . would, before long years were over our heads, be infinitely more painful." He declares that he is hemmed in by all sorts of difficulties. " Nevertheless the path has shown itself a fair one, neither more difficult nor less so than most paths in life in which a man of energy may hope to do much if he believes in himself, and is at peace within." Thus relieved in mind, he makes his decision in spite of adverse fate. " My course of life is taken, I will not leave London — I will make myself a name and a position as well as an income by some kind of pursuit connected with science which is the thing for which Nature has fitted me if she has ever fitted any one for anything."

But suddenly the long wait, the faith in self, were justified, and the turning point came. "There is always a Cape Horn in one's life that one either weathers or wrecks one's self on," he writes to his sister. " Thank God, I think I may say I have weathered mine — not without a good deal of damage to spars and rigging though, for it blew deuced hard on the other side." In 1854 a permanent Lecture- lecture-ship was offered him at the Government ahips School of Mines; also, a lectureship at St. Thomas' Hospital; and he was asked to give various other lecture courses. He thus found himself able to establish the home for which he had waited eight years. In July, 1855, he was married to Miss Heathorn.

The succeeding years from 1855 to 1860 were filled with various kinds of work connected with science: original investigation, printing of monographs, and estab-lishing of natural history museums. His advice concerning local museums is inter-esting and characteristically expressed. "It [the local museum if properly arranged] will tell both natives and strangers exactly what they want to know, and possess great scientific interest and importance. Whereas the ordinary lumber-room of clubs from New Zealand, Hindu idols, sharks' teeth, mangy monkeys, scorpions, and conch shells — who shall describe the weary inutility of it? It is really worse than nothing, because it leads the unwary to look for objects of science elsewhere than under their noses. What they want to know is that their America is here,' as Wilhelm Meister has it." During this period, also, he began his lectures to working-men, calling them Peoples' Lectures. "*Popular* lectures," he said, "I hold to be an abomination unto the Lord." Working-men attended these lectures in great num-bers, and to them Huxley seemed to be always able to speak at his best. His purpose in giving these lectures should be expressed in his own words: " I want the working class to understand that Science and her ways are great facts for them — that physical virtue is the base of all other, and that they are to be] clean and temperate and all the rest — not because fellows in black and white ties tell them so, but because there are plain and patent laws which they must obey ' under pen-alties.'"

Toward the close of 1859, Darwin's " Origin of Species " was published. It raised a great outcry in England; and Huxley immediately came forward as chief de- Attitude fender of the faith therein set forth. He took toward part in debates on this subject, the most famous of which was the one between himself and Bishop Wilberforce at Oxford. The Bishop concluded his speech by turning to Huxley and asking, "Was it through his grandfather or grandmother that he claimed descent from a monkey?" Huxley, as is reported by an eye-witness, " slowly and deliberately arose. A slight tall figure, stern and pale, very quiet and grave, he stood before us and spoke those tremendous words. ... He was not ashamed to have a monkey for an ancestor; but he would be ashamed to be connected with a man who used great gifts to obscure the truth." Another story indicates the temper of that time. Carlyle, whose writing had strongly influenced Huxley, and whom Huxley had come to know, could not forgive him for his attitude toward evolution. One day, years after the publication of *Man's Place in Nature,* Huxley, seeing Carlyle on the other side of the street, a broken pathetic figure, walked over and spoke to him. The old man merely remarked, " You 're Huxley, are n't you ? the man that says we are all descended from monkeys," and passed on. Huxley, however, saw nothing degrading to man's dignity in the theory of evolution. In a wonderfully fine sentence he gives his own estimate of the theory as it affects man's future on earth. " Thoughtful men once escaped from the blinding influences of traditional prejudices, will find in the lowly stock whence man has sprung the best evidence of the splendour of his capacities; and will discover, in his long progress through the past, a reasonable ground of faith in his attainment of a nobler future." As a result of all these controversies on *The Origin of Species* and of investigations to uphold Darwin's theory, Huxley wrote his first book, already mentioned, *Man's Place in Nature.*

To read a list of the various kinds of work which Hux-ley was doing from 1870 to 1875 is to be convinced of his Eathifsh- abundant energy and many interests. At about ment of this time Huxley executed the plan which he tories had had in mind for a long time, the establishment of laboratories for the use of students. His object was to furnish a more exact preliminary training. He complains that the student who enters the medical school is "so habituated to learn only from books, or oral teaching, that the attempt to learn from things and to get his know ledge at first hand is something new and strange." To make this method of teaching successful in the schools, Huxley gave practical instruction in laboratory work to school-masters.

"If I am to be remembered at all," Huxley once wrote, "I would rather it should be as a man who did his best to help the people than by any other title." Certainly as much of his time as could be spared from his regular work was given to help others. His lectures to workingmen and school-masters have already been mentioned. In addition, he lectured to women on physiology and to children on elementary science. In order to be of greater service to the children, Huxley, in spite of delicate health, became a member of the London School Board. His immediate object was " to temper book-learning with something Service to of the direct knowledge of Nature." His other pur-women and poses were to secure a better physical training for children and to give them a clearer understanding of social and moral law. He did not believe, on the one hand, in overcrowding the curriculum, but, on the other hand, he felt that all education should be thrown open to all that bach man might know to what state in life he was called" [Another statement of his purpose and beliefs is given by Professor Gladstone, who says of his work on the board: He resented the idea that schools were to train either congregations for churches or hands for factories. He was on the Board as a friend of children. What he sought to do for the child was for the child's sake, that it might live a fuller, truer, worthier life."

The immense amount of work which Huxley did in these years told very seriously on his naturally weak con-stitution. It became necessary for him finally vacations for two successive years to stop work altogether. abroad. In 1872 he went to the Mediterranean and to Egypt. This was a holiday full of interest for a man like Huxley who looked upon the history of the world and man's place in the world with a keen scientific mind. Added to this sci-entific bent of mind, moreover, Huxley had a deep appre-ciation for the picturesque in nature and life. Bits of de-scription indicate his enjoyment in this vacation. He writes of his entrance to the Mediterra-nean, "It was a lovely morning, and nothing could be grander than Ape Hill on one side and the Rock on the other, looking like great lions or sphinxes on each side of a gateway." In Cairo, Huxley found much to interest him in archaeology, geology, and the every-day life of the streets. At the end of a month, he writes that he is very well and very grateful to Old Nile for all that he has done for him, not the least " for a whole universe of new thoughts and pictures of life." The trip, however, did no lasting good. In 1873 Huxley was again very ill, but was under such heavy costs at this time that another vacation was impossible. At this moment, a critical one in his life, some of his close scientific friends placed to his credit twenty-one hundred pounds to enable him to take the much needed rest. Darwin wrote to Huxley concerning the gift: "In doing this we are convinced that we act for the public interest." He assured Huxley that the friends who gave this felt toward him as a brother. "I am sure that you will return this feeling and will therefore be glad to give us the opportunity of aiding you in some degree, as this will be a happiness to us to the last day of our lives." The gift made it possible for Huxley to take another long vacation, part of which was spent with Sir Joseph Hooker, a noted English botanist, visiting the volcanoes of Auvergne. After this trip he steadily improved in health, with no other serious illness for ten years.

In 1876 Huxley was invited to visit America and to deliver the inaugural address at Johns Hopkins University. In July of this year accordingly, in company with his wife, he crossed to New York. Everywhere Huxley was received with enthusiasm, for his name was a very familiar one. Two quotations from his address at Johns Hopkins are especially worthy of attention as a part of his message to Americans. "It has been my fate to see great educational funds fossilise into mere bricks and mortar in the petrifying springs of architecture, with nothing left to work them. A great warrior is said to have made a desert and called it peace. Trustees have sometimes made a palace and called it a university."

The second quotation is as follows: —

I cannot say that I am in the slightest degree impressed by your bigness or your material resources, as such. Size is not grandeur, territory does not make a nation. The great issue, about which hangs true sublimity, and the terror of overhanging fate, is. what are you going to do with all these things ? . . .

The one condition of success, your sole safeguard, is the moral worth and intellectual clearness of the individual citizen. Education cannot give these, but it can cherish them and bring them to the front in whatever station of society they are to be found, and the universities ought to be, and may be, the fortresses of the higher life of the nation.

After the return from America, the same innumerable occupations were continued. It would be impossible in short space even to enumerate all Huxley's various publications of the next ten years. His work, however, changed gradually from scientific investigation to administrative work, not the least important of which wass the office of Inspector of Fisheries. A second important office was the Presidency of the Royal Society. Of the work of this society Sir Joseph Hooker writes: "The duties of the office are manifold and heavy; they include attendance at all the meetings of the Fellows, and of the councils, committees, and sub-committees of the Society, and especially the supervision of the printing and illustrating all papers on biological subjects that are published in the Society's Transactions and Proceedings; the latter often involving a protracted correspondence with the authors. To this must be added a share in the supervision of the staff officers, of the library and correspondence, and the details of house-keeping." All the work connected with this and many other offices bespeaks a life too hard-driven and accounts fully for the continued ill-health which finally resulted in a complete break-down.

Huxley had always advocated that the age of sixty was the time for "official death," and had looked forward to a peaceful "Indian summer." With this object puranit in mind and troubled by increasing ill-health, he of began in **1885** to give up his work. But to live even in comparative idleness, after so many years of activity, was difficult. " I am sure," he says, " that the habit of incessant work into which we all drift is as bad in its way as dram-drinking. In time you cannot be comfortable without stimulus." But continued bodily weakness told upon him to the extent that all work became distasteful. An utter weariness with frequent spells of the blues took possession of him; and the story of his life for some years is the story of the long pursuit of health in England, Switzerland, and especially in Italy.

Although Huxley was wretchedly ill during this period, he wrote letters which are good to read for their humor and for their pictures of foreign cities. Rome he writes of as an idle, afternoony sort of place from which it is difficult to depart. He worked as eagerly over the historic remains in Borne as he would over a collection of geological specimens. " I begin to understand Old Borne pretty well and I am quite learned in the Catacombs, which suit me, as a kind of Christian fossils out of which one can reconstruct the body of the primitive Church." Florence, for a man with a conscience and ill-health, had too many picture galleries. "They are a sore burden to the conscience if you don't go to see them, and an awful trial to the back and legs if you do," he complained. He found Florence, nevertheless, a lovely place and full of most interesting things to see and do. His letters with reference to himself also are vigorously and entertainingly expressed. He writes in a characteristic way of his growing difficulty with his hearing. " It irritates me not to hear; it irritates me still more to be spoken to as if I were deaf, and the absurdity of being irritated on the last ground irritates me still more." And again he writes in a more hopeful strain, " With fresh air and exercise an careful avoidance of cold and night air I am to be all right again." He then adds: "l am not fond of coddling; but as Paddy gave his pig the best corner in his cabin — because 'shure, he paid the rint'—I feel bound to take care of myself as a household animal of value, to say nothing of other points."

Although he was never strong after this long illness, Huxley began in 1889 to be much better. The first sign (Last years) of returning vigor was the eagerness with which he entered into a controversy with Gladstone. Huxley had always enjoyed a mental battle; and some of his fiercest tilts were with Gladstone. He even found the cause of better health in this controversy, and was grateful to the " Grand Old Man " for making home happy for him. From this time to his death, Huxley wrote a number of articles on politics, science, and religion, many of which were published in the volume called *Controverted Questions.* The main value of these essays lies in the fact that Huxley calls upon men to give clear reasons for the faith which they claim as theirs, and makes, as a friend wrote of him, hazy thinking and slovenly, half-formed conclusions seem the base thing they really are.

The last years of Huxley's life were indeed the longed-for Indian summer. Away from the noise of London at Eastbourne by the sea, he spent many happy hours with old-time friends and in his garden, which was a great joy to him. His large family of sons and daughters and grand-children brought much cheer to his last days. Almost to the end he was working and writing for publication. Three days before his death he wrote to his old friend, Hooker, that he did n't feel at all like " sending in his checks " and hoped to recover. He died very quietly on June 29,1895. That he met death with the same calm faith and strength with which he had met life is indicated by the lines which his wife wrote and which he requested to be his epitaph: —

Be not afraid, ye waiting hearts that weep ; For still He giveth His beloved sleep, And if an endless sleep He wills, so best

To attempt an analysis of Huxley's character, unique and baffingly complex as it is, is beyond the scope of this sketch; but to give only the mere faets of his life is to do an injustice to the vivid personality of the man as it is revealed in his letters. All his human interest (Huxley's human interest) in people and things —pets, and flowers, and family—brightens many pages of the two ponderous volumes. Now one reads of his grief over some backward-going plant, or over some garden tragedy, as " A lovely clematis in full flower, which I had spent hours in nailing up, has just died suddenly. I am more inconsolable than Jonah" Now one is amused with a nonsense letter to one of his children, and again with an account of a pet. "I wish you would write seriously to M—. She is not behaving well to Oliver. I have seen handsomer kittens, but few more lively, and energetically destructive. Just now he scratched away at something M—says cost 13s. 6*d*. a yard and reduced more or less of it to combings. M—therefore excludes him from the dining-room and all those opportunities of higher education which he would have in *my* house." Frequently one finds a description of some event, so vividly done that the mere reading of it seems like a real experience. An account of Tennyson's burial in Westminster is a typical bit of description: —

Bright sunshine streamed through the windows of the nave, while the choir was in half gloom, and as each shaft of light illuminated the flower-covered bier as it slowly travelled on, one thought of the bright succession of his works between the dark-ness before and the darkness after. I am glad to say that the Royal Society was represented by four of its chief officers, and nine of the commonalty, including myself. Tennyson has a right to that, as the first poet since Lucretius who has understood the drift of science.

No parts of the *Life and Letters* are more enjoyable than those concerning the " Happy Family " as a friend (Family life) of Huxley's names his household. His family of seven children found their father a most engaging friend and companion. He could tell them wonderful sea stories and animal stories and could draw fascinating pictures. His son writes of how when he was ill with scarlet fever he used to look forward to his father's home-coming. " The solitary days — for I was the first victim in the family — were very long, and I looked forward with intense interest to one half-hour after dinner, when he would come up and draw scenes from the history of a remarkable bull-terrier and his family that went to the seaside in a most human and child-delighting manner. I have seldom suffered a greater disappointment than when, one evening, I fell asleep just before this fairy half-hour, and lost it out of my life."

The account of the comradeship between Huxley and his wife reads like a good old-time romance. He was attracted to her at first by her " simplicity and directness united with an unusual degree of cultivation," Huxley's son writes. On her he depended for advice in his work, and for companionship at home and abroad when wandering in search of health in Italy and Switzerland. When he had been separated from her for some time, he wrote, " Nobody, children or anyone else, can be to me what you are. Ulysses preferred his old woman to immortality, and this absence has led me to see that he was as wise in that as in other things." Again he writes," Against all trouble (and I have had my share) I weigh a wife-comrade ' trew and fest' in all emergencies."

The letters also give one a clear idea of the breadth of Huxley's interests, particularly of his appreciation of the various forms of art. Huxley believed strongly in the arts as a refining and helpful influence in tion of education. He keenly enjoyed good music. Pro-fessor Hewes writes of him that one breaking in upon him; in the afternoon at South Kensington would not infre-' quently be met " with a snatch of some melody of Bach's ' fugue." He also liked good pictures, and always had among his friends well-known artists, as Alma-Tadema, Sir Frederick Leighton, and Burne-Jones. He read poetry widely, and strongly advocated the teaching of poetry in English schools. As to poetry, his own preferences are interesting. Wordsworth he considered too discursive; Shelley was too diffuse; Keats, he liked for pure beauty, Browning for strength, and Tennyson for his understanding of modern science; but most frequently of all he read Milton and Shakespeare.

As to Huxley's appearance, and as to the impression which his personality made upon others, the description of a friend, Mr. G. W. Smalley, presents him Personality with striking force. " The square forehead, the square jaw, the tense lines of the mouth, the deep flashing dark eyes, the impression of something more than strength he gave you, an impression of sincerity, of solid force, of immovability, yet with the gentleness arising from the serene consciousness of his strength — all this belonged to Huxley and to him alone. The first glance magnetized his audience. The eyes were those of one accustomed to command, of one having authority, and not fearing on occasion to use it. The hair swept carelessly away from the broad forehead and grew rather long behind, yet the length did not suggest, as it often does, effeminacy. He was masculine in everything — look, gesture, speech. Sparing of gesture, sparing of emphasis, careless of mere rhetorical or oratorical art, he had nevertheless the secret of the highest art of all, whether in Oratory or whatever else — he had simplicity."

Simplicity, directness, sincerityl—all these qualities describe Huxley; hut the one attribute which distinguishes | distin him above all others is love of truth A love of guishing truth, as the phrase characterizes Huxley, would necessarily produce a scholarly habit of mind. It was the zealous search for truth which determined his method of work. In science, Huxley would " take at second hand nothing for which he vouched in teaching." Some one reproached him for wasting time verifying what another had already done. " If that is his practice," he commented, "his work will never live." The same motive made him a master of languages. To be able to read at first hand the writings of other nations, he learned German, French, Italian, and Greek. One of the chief reasons for learning to read Greek was to see for himself if Aristotle really did say that the heart had only three chambers—an error, he discovered, not of Aristotle, but of the translator. It was, moreover, the scholar in Huxley which made him impatient of narrow, half-formed, foggy conclusions. His own work has all the breadth and freedom and universality of the scholar, but it has, also, a quality equally distinctive of the scholar, namely, an infinite precision in the matter of detail.

If love of truth made Huxley a scholar, it made him, also, a courageous fighter. Man's first duty, as he saw it, A coura *was to seek the truth; his second was to teach* cm *it to others, and, if necessary, to contend valiantly fightar for it To fail to teach what you honestly know to be true, because it may harm your reputation, or even because it may give pain to others, is cowardice. "I am not greatly concerned about any reputation," Huxley writes ' to his wife, " except that of being entirely honest and straightforward." Regardless of warnings that the publica-tion of* Man's Place in Nature would ruin his career, Huxley passed on to others what nature had revealed to him. He was regardless, also, of the confusion and pain which his view would necessarily bring to those who had been nourished in old traditions. To stand with a man or two and to do battle with the world on the score of its old beliefs, has never been an easy task since the world began. Certainly it required fearlessness and determination to wrestle with the prejudices against science in the middle of the nineteenth century — how much may be gathered from the reading of Darwin's *Life and Letters*. The attitude of the times toward science has already been indicated. One may be allowed to give one more example from the reported address of a clergyman. " O ye men of science, ye men of science, leave us our ancestors in paradise, and you may have yours in Zoological gardens." The war was, for the most part, between the clergy and the men of science, but it is necessary to remember that Huxley fought not against Christianity, but against dogma; that he fought not against the past, — he had great reverence for the accomplishment of the past, — but against unwillingness to accept the new truth of the present.

A scholar of the highest type and a fearless defender el true and honest thinking, Huxley certainly was: but the quality which gives meaning to his work, which A SCHALAR makes it live, is a certain human quality due to of the highest the fact that Huxley was always keenly alive to type the relation of science to the problems of life. For this reason, he was not content with the mere acquirement of knowledge; and for this reason, also, he could not quietly wait until the world should come to his way of thinking. Much of the time, therefore, which he would otherwise naturally have spent in research, he spent in contending for and in endeavoring to popularize the facts of science. It was this desire to make his ideas prevail that led Huxley to work for a mastery of the technique of speaking and writing. He hated both, but taught himself to do both well. The end of all his infinite pains about his writing was not because style for its own sake is worth while, but because he saw that the only way to win men to a consideiation of his message was to make it perfectly clear and attractive to them. Huxley's message to the people was that happiness, usefulness, and even material prosperity depend upon an understanding of the laws of nature. He also taught that a knowledge of the facts of science is the soundest basis for moral law; that a clear sense of the penalties which Nature inflicts for disobedience of her laws must eventually be the greatest force for the purification of life. If he was to be remembered, therefore, he desired that he should be remembered primarily as one who had helped the people " to think truly and to live rightly." Huxley's writing is, then, something more than a scholarly exposition of abstruse matter; for it has been further devoted to the increasing of man's capacity for usefulness, and to the betterment of his life here on earth.

II
SUBJECT-MATTER, STRUCTURE, AND STYLE

From the point of view of subject-matter, structure, and style, Huxley's essays are admirably adapted to the uses of the student in English. The themes of the essays are two, education and science. In these two subjects and Huxley earnestly sought to arouse interest and to impart knowledge, because he believed that intelligence in these matters is essential for the advancement of the race in strength and morality. Both subjects, therefore, should be valuable to the student. In education, certainly, he should be interested, since it is his main occupation, if not his chief concern. Essays like *A Liberal Education* and *The Principal Subjects of Education* may suggest to him the meaning of all his work, and may suggest, also, the things which it would be well for him to know; and, even more, a consideration of these subjects may arouse him to a greater interest and responsibility than he usually assumes toward his own mental equipment. Of greater interest probably will be the subjects which deal with nature; for the ways of nature are more nearly within the range of his real concerns than are the wherefores of study. The story of the formation of a piece of chalk, the substance which lies at the basis of all life, the habits of sea animals, are all subjects the nature of which is akin to his own eager interest in the world.

Undoubtedly the subjects about which Huxley writes will "appeal" to the student; but it is in analysis that the real discipline lies,. For analysis Huxley's essays are excellent. They illustrate "the clear power of exposition," and such power is, as Huxley wrote to Tyndall, the one quality the people want,— exposition "so clear that they may think they understand even if they don't." Huxley obtains that perfect clearness in his own work by simple definition, by keeping steadily before his clearnass audience his intention, and by making plain by simple throughout his lecture a well-defined organic structure. No X-ray machine is needful to make the skeleton visible; it stands forth with the parts all nicely related and compactly joined. In reference to structure, his son and biographer writes, " He loved to visualize his object clearly. The framework of what he wished to say would always be drawn out first." Professor Ray Lankester also mentions Huxley's love of form. "He deals with form not only as a mechanical engineer *in partibus* (Huxley's own description of himself), but also as an artist, a born lover of form, a character which others recognize in him though he does not himself set it down in his analysis." Huxley's own account of his efforts to shape his work is suggestive. " The fact is that I have a great love and respect for my native tongue, and take great pains to use it properly. Sometimes I write essays half-a-dozen times before I can get them into proper shape; and I believe I become more fastidious as I grow older." And, indeed, there is a marked difference in firmness of structure between the earlier essays, such as *On the Educational Value of the Natural History Sciences, written,* as Huxley acknowledges, in great haste, and the later essays, such as *A Liberal Education* and *The Method of Scientific Investigation.* To trace and to define this difference will be most helpful to the student who is building up a knowledge of structure for his own use.

According to Huxley's biographer in the *Life and Letters of Thomas Henry Huxley,* the essays which represent him at his best are those published in 1868. They are A Piece of Chalky *A Liberal Education,* and *On the Physical Basis of Life,* In connection with the comment on these essays is the following quotation which gives one interesting information as to Huxley's method of obtaining a clear style : —

This lecture on *A Piece of Chalk* together with two others de-livered this year, seems to me to mark the maturing of his style into that mastery of clear expression for which he deliberately labored, the saying exactly what he meant, neither too much nor too little, without confusion and without obscurity. Have something to say, and say it. was the of Wellington's theory of style Huxley's was to say that which has to be said m such language that you can stand cross-examination on each word. Be clear, though you may be convicted of error. If you are clearly wrong, you will run up against a fact sometime and get set right. If you shuffle with your subject, and study chiefly to use, language which will give a loophole of escape either way, there is no hope for you.

This was the secret of his lucidity. In no one could Buffon's aphorism on style find a better illustration, Le style c'est l' homms méme. In him science and literature, too often divorced, were closely united; and literature owes him a debt for importing into it so much of the highest scientific habit of mind; for showing that truthfulness need not be bald, and that real power lies more in exaet accuracy than in luxuriance of diction.

Huxley's own theory as to how clearness is to be obtained gets at the root of the matter. " For my part, I venture to doubt the wisdom of attempting to mould one's style by any other process than that of striving after the clear and forcible expression of definite conceptions; in which process the Glaseian precept, first catch your definite conception, is probably the most difficult to obey." Perfect clearness, above every other quality of style, certainly is characteristic of Huxley; but clearness alone other does not make subject-matter literature. In addition to this quality, Huxley's writing wins the of style reader by the racy diction, the homely illustration, the plain, honest phrasing. All these and other qualities bring one into an intimate relationship with his subject. A man of vast technical learning, he is still so interested in the relation of his facts to the problems of men that he is always able to infuse life into the driest of subjects, in other words, to *humanize* his knowledge; and in the estimation of Matthew Arnold, this is the true work of the scholar, the highest mission of style.

III
SUGGESTED STUDIES IN SUBJECT-MATTER, STRUCTURE, AND STYLE

Although fully realizing that the questions here given are only such as are generally used everywhere by instructors in English, the editor has, nevertheless, included them with the hope that some one may find them helpful.

The studies given include a few general questions and suggestions on subject-matter, structure, and style. The questions on structure are based on an analysis of the whole composition and of the paragraph; those on style are based on a study of sentences and words. Such a division of material may seem unwarranted; for, it may be urged, firmness of structure depends, to a certain extent, upon sentence-form and words; and clearness of style, to a large extent, upon the form of the paragraph and whole .composition. The two, certainly, cannot be in justice separated and especially is it true, more deeply true than the average student can be brought to believe, that structure, " mind, in style " as Pater phrases it, primarily determines not only clearness, but also such qualities of style as reserve, refinement, and simple Doric beauty. Since, however, structure is more obviously associated with the larger groups, and style with the smaller, the questions have been arranged according to this division.

I. Suggestions for the Study of Subjeot-Matter.

1. To whom does Huxley address the essay? 2. Can you see any adaptation of his material to his audience? 3. How would *A Piece of Chalk* be differently presented if given before a science club? 4. Does Huxley make his subject interesting? If so, how does he accomplish this? 5. Is the personality of Huxley suggested by the essays? See *Life and Letter*, vol. ii, p. 298.

II. Suggestions for the Study of Structure.

A.*Analysis of the whole composition.*

1. State in one complete sentence the theme of the essay. 2. Analyze the essay for the logical development of the thought.

a . Questions on the Introduction.

In the introduction, how does the author approach his material? Does he give the main points of the essay? Does he give his reasons for writing? Does he narrow his subject to one point of view? Is the introduction a digression?

b . Questions on the Body.

Can you find large groups of thought? Are these groups closely related to the theme and to each other? Do you find any digressions? Is the method used in developing the groups inductive or deductive? Is the method different in different groups? Are the groups arranged for good emphasis in the whole composition?

c . Questions on the Conclusion.

How does the author conclude the essay? Does the conclusion sum up the points of the essay? Are any new points suggested? Is the thought of the whole essay stated? Do you consider it a strong conclusion?

8. Make out an outline which shall picture the skeleton of the essay studied. In

making the outline express the topics in the form of complete statements, phrase the thought for clear sequence, and be careful about such matters as spacing and punctuation.

B. Analysis of paragraph structure.

1. Can a paragraph be analyzed in the same manner as the whole composition? 2. Can you express the thought of each paragraph in a complete sentence? 8. Can you find different points presented in the paragraph developing the paragraph topic, as the large groups of the whole composition develop the theme? 4 Are the paragraphs closely related, and how are they bound together? 5. Can any of the paragraphs be combined to advantage? 6. Read from Barrett Wendell's *English Composition* the chapter on paragraphs. Are Hurley's paragraphs constructed in accordance with the principles given in this chapter? 7. Is the paragraph type varied? For paragraph types, see Scott and Denny's *Paragraph Writing*.

C. Comparative study of the structure of the essay.

1. Do you find any difference between Huxley's earlier and later essays as regards the structure of the whole, or the structure of the paragraph? 2. Which essay seems to you to be most successful in structure? 8. Has the character of the audience any influence upon the structure of the essays? 4. Compare the structure of one of Huxley's essays with that of some other essay recently studied. 5. Has the nature of the material any influence upon the structure of the essay?

III. Suggestions for the Study of Style.

A. Exactly what do you mean by style?

B. Questions on sentence structure.

1. From any given essay, group together sentences which are long, short, loose, periodic, balanced, simple, compound ; note those peculiar, for any reason, to Huxley. 2. Stevenson says, " The one rule is to be infinitely various; to interest, to disappoint, to surprise and still to gratify; to be ever changing, as it were, the stitch, and yet still to give the effect of ingenious neatness."

Do Huxley's sentences conform to Stevenson's rule? Compare Huxley's sentences with Stevenson's for variety in form. Is there any reason for the difference between the form of the two writers? 8. Does this quotation from Pater's essay on *Style* describe Huxley's sentences? "The blithe, crisp sentence, decisive as a child's expression of its needs, may alternate with the long-contending, victoriously intricate sentence; the sentence, born with the integrity of a single word, relieving the sort of sentence in which, if you look closely, you can see contrivance, much adjustment, to bring a highly qualified matter into compass at one view." 4. How do Huxley's sentences compare with those of Ruskin, or with those of any author recently studied? 5. Are Huxley's sentences musical? How does an author make his sentences musical?

C. Questions on words.

1. Do you find evidence of exactness, a quality which Huxley said he labored for? 2. Are the words general or specific in character? 8. How does Huxley make his subject-matter attractive? 4. From what sources does Huxley derive his words? Are they every-day words, or more scholarly in character? 5. Do you find any figures? Are these mainly ornamental or do they reinforce the thought? 6. Are there many allusions and quotations? Can you easily recognize the source? 7. Pater says in his essay on Style that the literary artist "begets a vocabulary faithful to the colouring of his own spirit, and in the strictest sense original." Do you find that Huxley's vocabulary suggests the man? 8. Does Huxley seem to search for " the smooth, or win-some, or forcible word, as such, or quite simply and honestly, for the word's adjustment to its meaning"? 9. Make out a list of the words and proper names in any given essay which are not familiar to you; write out the explanation of these in the form of notes giving any information which is interesting and relevant.

D. General question on style.

1. How is Huxley's style adapted to the subject-matter 2. Can you explain the difference in style of the different essays by the difference in purpose? 3. Compare Huxley's way of saying things with some other author's way of saying things. 4. Huxley says of his essays to workingmen, " I only wish I had had the sense to anticipate the run these have had here and abroad, and I would have revised them properly. As they stand they are terribly in the rough, from a literary point of view." Do you find evidences of roughness?

THOMAS HENRY HUXLEY
AUTOBIOGRAPHY

And when I consider, in one view, the many things . . . which I have upon my hands, I feel the burlesque of being employed in this manner at my time of life. But, in another view, and taking in all circumstances, these things, as trifling as they may appear, no less than things of greater importance, seem to be put upon me to do. — *Bishop Butter to the Duchess of Somerset.*

THE "many things" to which the Duchess's corre-spondent here refers are the repairs and improvements of the episcopal seat at Auckland. I doubt if the great apologist, greater in nothing than in the simple dignity of his character, would have considered the writing an account of himself as a thing which could be put upon him to do whatever circumstances might be taken in. But the good bishop lived in an age when a man might write books and yet be permitted to keep his private existence to himself; in the pre-Boswellian epoch, when the germ of the photographer lay concealed in the distant future, and the interviewer who pervades our age was an unforeseen, indeed unimaginable, birth of time.

At present, the most convinced believer in the aphorism " Bene qui latuit, bene vixit," is not always able to act up to it. An importunate person informs him that his portrait is about to be published and will be accompanied by a biography which the importunate person proposes to write. The sufferer knows what that means; either he undertakes to revise the " biography " or he does not. In the former case, he makes himself responsible; in the latter, he allows the publication of a mass of more or less fulsome inaccuracies for which he will be held responsible by those who are familiar with the prevalent art of self-advertisement. On the whole, it may be better to get over the " burlesque of being employed in this manner " and do the thing himself.

It was by reflections of this kind that, some years ago, I was led to write and permit the publication of the subjoined sketch.

I was born about eight o'clock in the morning on the 4th of May, 1825, at Ealing, which was, at that time, as quiet a little country village as could be found within a half-a-dozen miles of Hyde Park Corner. Now it is a suburb of London with, I believe, 30,000 inhabitants. My father was one of the masters in a large semi-public school which at one time had a high reputation. I am not aware that any portents preceded my arrival in this world, but, in my childhood, I remember hearing a traditional account of the manner in which I lost the chance of an endowment of great practical value. The windows of my mother's room were open, in consequence of the unusual warmth of the weather. For the same reason, probably, a neighbouring beehive had swarmed, and the new colony, pitching on the window-sill, was making its way into the room when the horrified nurse shut down the sash. If that well-meaning woman had only abstained from her ill-timed interference, the swarm might have settled on my lips, and I should have been endowed with that mellifluous eloquence which, in this country, leads far more surely than worth, capacity, or honest work, to the highest places in Church and State. But the opportunity was lost, and I have been obliged to content myself through life with saying what I mean in the plainest of plain language, than which, I suppose, there is no habit more ruinous to a man's prospects of advancement.

Why I was christened Thomas Henry I do not know; but it is a curious chance that my parents should have fixed for my usual denomination upon the name of that particular Apostle with whom I have always felt most sympathy. Physically and mentally I am the son of my mother so completely — even down to peculiar movements of the hands, which made their appearance in me as I reached the age she had when I noticed them — that I can hardly find any trace of my father in myself, except an inborn faculty for drawing, which unfortunately, in my case, has never been cultivated, a hot temper, and that amount of tenacity of purpose which unfriendly observers sometimes call obstinacy.

My mother was a slender brunette, of an emotional and energetic temperament, and possessed of the most piercing black eyes I ever saw in a woman's head. With no more education than other women of the middle classes in her day, she had an excellent mental capacity. Her most distinguishing characteristic, however, was rapidity of thought. If one ventured to suggest she had not taken much time to arrive at any conclusion, she would say, "I cannot help it, things flash across me." That peculiarity has been passed on to me in full strength; it has often stood me in good stead; it has sometimes played me sad tricks, and it has always been a danger. But, after all, if my time were to come over again, there is nothing I would less willingly part with than my inheritance of mother wit.

I have next to nothing to say about my childhood. In later years my mother, looking at me almost reproachfully, would sometimes say, "Ah! you were such a pretty boy!" whence I had no difficulty in concluding that I had not fulfilled my early promise in the matter of looks. In fact, I have a distinct recollection of certain curls of which I was vain, and of a conviction that I closely resembled that handsome, courtly gentleman, Sir Herbert Oakley, who was vicar of our parish, and who was as a god to us country folk, because he was occasionally visited by the then Prince George of Cambridge. I remember turning my pinafore wrong side forwards in order to represent a surplice, and preaching to my mother's maids in the kitchen as nearly as possible in Sir Herbert's manner one Sunday morning when the rest of the family were at church. That is the earliest indication I can call to mind of the strong clerical affinities which my friend Mr. Herbert Spencer has always ascribed to me, though I fancy they have for the most part remained in a latent state.

My regular school training was of the briefest, perhaps fortunately, for though my way of life has made me acquainted with all sorts and conditions of men, from the highest to the lowest, I deliberately affirm that the society I fell into at school was the worst I have ever known. We boys were average lads, with much the same inherent capacity for good and evil as any others; but the people who were set over us cared about as much for our intellectual and moral welfare as if they were baby-farmers. We were left to the operation of the struggle for existence among ourselves, and bullying was the least of the ill practices current among us. Almost the only cheerful reminiscence in connection with the place which arises in my mind is that of a battle I had with one of my classmates, who had bullied me until I could stand it no longer. I was a very slight lad, but there was a wild-cat element in me which, when roused, made up for lack of weight, and I licked my adversary effectually. However, one of my first experiences of the extremely rough-and-ready nature of justice, as exhibited by the course of things in general, arose out of the fact that I — the victor — had a black eye, while he — the vanquished — had none, so that I got into disgrace and he did not. We made it up, and thereafter I was unmolested. One of the greatest shocks I ever received in my life was to be told a dozen years afterwards by the groom who brought me my horse in a stable-yard in Sydney that he was my quondam antagonist. He had a long story of family misfortune to account for his position, but at that time it was necessary to deal very cautiously with mysterious strangers in New South Wales, and on inquiry I found that the unfortunate young man had not only been "sent out," but had undergone more than one colonial con-viction.

As I grew older, my great desire was to be a me-chanical engineer, but the fates were against this and, while very young, I commenced the study of medicine under a medical brother-in-law. But, though the Institute of Mechanical Engineers would certainly not own me, I am not sure that I have not all along been a sort of mechanical engineer *in partibus infidelium*. I am now occasionally horrified to think how very little I ever knew or cared about medicine as the art of healing. The only part of my professional course which really and deeply interested me was physiology, which is the mechanical engineering of living machines; and, notwithstanding that natural science has been my proper business, I am afraid there is very little of the genuine naturalist in me. I never collected anything, and species work was always a burden to me; what I cared for was the architectural and engineering part of the business, the working out of the wonderful unity of plan in the thousands and thousands of diverse living constructions, and the modifications of similar apparatuses to serve diverse ends. The extraordinary attraction I felt towards the study of the intricacies of living structure nearly proved fatal to me at the outset. I was a mere boy — I think between thirteen and fourteen years of age — when I was taken by some older student friends of mine to the first *post-mortem* examination I ever attended. All my life I have been most unfortunately sensitive to the disagreeables which attend anatomical pursuits, but on this occasion my curiosity overpowered all other feelings, and I spent two or three hours in gratifying it. I did not cut myself, and none of the ordinary symptoms of dissection-poison supervened, but poisoned I was somehow, and I remember sinking into a strange state of apathy. By way of a last chance, I was sent to the care of some good, kind people, friends of my father's, who lived in a farmhouse in the heart of Warwick-shire. I remember staggering from my bed to the window on the bright spring morning after my arrival, and throwing open the casement. Life seemed to come back on the wings of the breeze, and to this day the faint odor of wood-smoke, like that which floated across the farm-yard in the early morning, is as good to me as the " sweet south upon a bed of violets." I soon recovered, but for years I suffered from occasional paroxysms of internal pain, and from that time my constant friend, hypochondriacal dyspepsia, commenced his half century of co-tenancy of my fleshly tabernacle.

Looking back on my " Lehrjahre," I am sorry to say that I do not think that any account of my doings as a student would tend to edification. In fact, I should distinctly warn ingenuous youth to avoid imitating my example. I worked extremely hard when it pleased me, and when it did not — which was a very frequent case — I was extremely idle (unless making caricatures of one's pastors and masters is to be called a branch of industry), or else wasted my energies in wrong directions. I read everything I could lay hands upon, including novels, and took up all sorts of pursuits to drop them again quite as speedily. No doubt it was very largely my own fault, but the only instruction from which I ever obtained the proper effect of education was that which I received from Mr. Wharton Jones, who was the lecturer on physiology at the Charing Cross School of Medicine. The extent and precision of his knowledge impressed me greatly, and the severe exactness of his method of lecturing was quite to my taste. I do not know that I have ever felt so much respect for anybody as a teacher before or since. I worked hard to obtain his approbation, and he was extremely kind and helpful to the youngster who, I am afraid, took up more of his time than he had any right to do. It was he who suggested the publication of my first scientific paper — a very little one — in the *Medical Gazette* of 1845, and most kindly corrected the literary faults which abounded in it, short as it was; for at that time, and for many years afterwards, I detested the trouble of writing, and would take no pains over it.

It was in the early spring of 1846, that, having finished my obligatory medical studies and passed the first M.D. examination at the London University, — though I was still too young to qualify at the College of Surgeons, — I was talking to a fellow-student (the present eminent physician, Sir Joseph Fayrer), and wondering what I should do to meet the imperative necessity for earning my own bread, when my friend suggested that I should write to Sir William Burnett, at that time Director-General for the Medical Service of the Navy, for an appointment. I thought this rather a strong thing to do, as Sir William was personally unknown to me, but my cheery friend would not listen to my scruples, so I went to my lodgings and wrote the best letter I could devise. A few days afterwards I received the usual official circular acknowledgment, but at the bottom there was written an instruction to call at Somerset House on such a day. I thought that looked like business, so at the appointed time I called and sent in my card, while I waited in Sir William's ante-room. He was a tall, shrewd-looking old gentleman, with a broad Scotch accent — and I think I see him now as he entered with my card in his hand. The first thing he did was to return it, with the frugal reminder that I should probably find it useful on some other occasion. The second was to ask whether I was an Irishman. I suppose the air of modesty about my appeal must have struck him. I satisfied the Director-General that I was English to the backbone, and he made some inquiries as to my student career, finally desiring me to hold myself ready for examination. Having passed this, I was in Her Majesty's Service, and entered on the books of Nelson's old ship, the *Victory*, for duty at Haslar Hospital, about a couple of months after I made my application.

My official chief at Haslar was a very remarkable person, the late Sir John Richardson, an excellent naturalist, and far-famed as an indomitable Arctic traveller. He was a silent, reserved man, outside the circle of his family and intimates; and, having a full share of youthful vanity, I was extremely disgusted to find that " Old John," as we irreverent youngsters called him, took not the slightest notice of my worshipful self either the first time I attended him, as it was my duty to do, or for some weeks afterwards. I am afraid to think of the lengths to which my tongue may have run on the subject of the churlishness of the chief, who was, in truth, one of the kindest-hearted and most considerate of men. But one day, as I was crossing the hospital square, Sir John stopped me, and heaped coals of fire on my head by telling me that he had tried to get me one of the resident appointments, much coveted by the assistant surgeons, but that the Admiralty had put in another man. "However," said he, " I mean to keep you here till I can get you something you will like," and turned upon his heel without waiting for the thanks I stammered out. That explained how it was I had not been packed off to the West Coast of Africa like some of my juniors, and why, eventually, I remained altogether seven months at Haslar.

After a long interval, during which "Old John" ignored my existence almost as completely as before, he stopped me again as we met in a casual way, and describing the service on which the *Rattlesnake* was likely to be employed, said that Captain Owen Stanley, who was to command the ship, had asked him to recommend an assistant surgeon who knew something of science; would I like that ? Of course I jumped at the offer. " Very well, I give you leave; go to London at once and see Captain Stanley." I went, saw my future commander, who was very civil to me, and promised to ask that I should be appointed to his ship, as in due time I was. It is a singular thing that, during the few months of my stay at Haslar, I had among my messmates two future Directors-General of the Medical Service of the Navy (Sir Alexander Armstrong and Sir John Watt-Reid), with the present President of the College of Physicians and my kindest of doctors, Sir Andrew Clark.

Life on board Her Majesty's ship in those days was a very different affair from what it is now, and ours was exceptionally rough, as we were often many months without receiving letters or seeing any civilised people but ourselves. In exchange, we had the interest of being about the last voyagers, I suppose, to whom it could be possible to meet with people who knew nothing of fire-arms — as we did on the south coast of New Guinea — and of making acquaintance with a variety of interesting savage and semi-civilised people. But, apart from experience of this kind and the opportunities offered for scientific work, to me, personally, the cruise was extremely valuable. It was good for me to live under sharp discipline; to be down on the realities of existence by living on bare necessaries; to find out how extremely well worth living life seemed to be when one woke up from a night's rest on a soft plank, with the sky for canopy and cocoa and weevilly biscuit the sole prospect for breakfast; and, more especially, to learn to work for the sake of what I got for myself out of it, even if it all went to the bottom and I along with it. My brother officers were as good fellows as sailors ought to be and generally are, but, naturally, they neither knew nor cared anything about my pursuits, nor understood why I should be so zealous in pursuit of the objects which my friends, the middies, christened "Buffons," after the title conspicuous on a volume of the *Suites d Buffon,* which stood on my shelf in the chart room.

During the four years of our absence, I sent home communication after communication to the " Linnean Society," with the same result as that obtained by Noah when he sent the raven out of his ark. Tired at last of hearing nothing about them, I determined to do or die, and in 1849 I drew up a more elaborate paper and forwarded it to the Royal Society. This was my dove, if I had only known it. But owing to the movements of the ship, I heard nothing of that either until my return to England in the latter end of the year 1850, when I found that it was printed and published, and that a huge packet of separate copies awaited me. When I hear some of my young friends complain of want of sympathy and encouragement, I am inclined to think that my naval life was not the least valuable part of my education.

Three years after my return were occupied by a battle between my scientific friends on the one hand and the Admiralty on the other, as to whether the latter ought, or ought not, to act up to the spirit of a pledge they had given to encourage officers who had done scientific work by contributing to the expense of publishing mine. At last the Admiralty, getting tired, I suppose, cut short the discussion by ordering me to join a ship, which thing I declined to do, and as Rastignac, in the Père Goriot *says to Paris, I said to London* " à nous deux." I desired to obtain a Professorship of either Physiology or Comparative Anatomy, and as vacancies occurred I applied, but in vain. My friend, Professor Tyndall, and I were candidates at the same time, he for the Chair of Physics and I for that of Natural History in the University of Toronto, which, fortunately, as it turned out, would not look at either of us. I say fortunately, not from any lack of respect for Toronto, but because I soon made up my mind that London was the place for me, and hence I have steadily declined the inducements to leave it, which have at various times been offered. At last, in 1854, on the translation of my warm friend Edward Forbes, to Edinburgh, Sir Henry de la Beche, the Director-General of the Geological Survey, offered me the post Forbes vacated of Paleontologist and Lecturer on Natural History. I refused the former point blank, and accepted the latter only provisionally, telling Sir Henry that I did not care for fossils, and that I should give up Natural History as soon as I could get a physio-logical post. But I held the office for thirty-one years, and a large part of my work has been paleontological. At that time I disliked public speaking, and had a firm conviction that I should break down every time I opened my mouth. I believe I had every fault a speaker could have (except talking at random or indulging in rhetoric), when I spoke to the first important audience I ever addressed, on a

Friday evening at the Royal Institution, in 1852. Yet, I must confess to having been guilty, malgré moi of as much public speaking as most of my contemporaries, and for the last ten years it ceased to be so much of a bugbear to me. I used to pity myself for having to go through this training, but I am now more disposed to compassionate the unfortunate audiences, especially my ever friendly hearers at the Royal Institution, who were the subjects of my oratorical experiments.

The last thing that it would be proper for me to do would be to speak of the work of my life, or to say at the end of the day whether I think I have earned my wages or not. Men are said to be partial judges of themselves. Young men may be, I doubt if old men are. Life seems terribly foreshortened as they look back and the mountain they set themselves to climb in youth turns out to be a mere spur of immeasurably higher ranges when, by failing breath, they reach the top. But if I may speak of the objects I have had more or less definitely in view since I began the ascent of my hillock, they are briefly these: To promote the increase of natural knowledge and to forward the application of scientific methods of investigation to all the problems of life to the best of my ability, in the conviction which has grown with my growth and strengthened with my strength, that there is no alleviation for the sufferings of mankind except veracity of thought and of action, and the resolute facing of the world as it is when the garment of make-believe by which pious hands have hidden its uglier features is stripped off.

It is with this intent that I have subordinated any reasonable, or unreasonable, ambition for scientific fame which I may have permitted myself to entertain to other ends; to the popularization of science; to the development and organisation of scientific education; to the endless series of battles and skirmishes over evolution; and to untiring opposition to that ecclesiastical spirit, that clericalism, which in England, as everywhere else, and to whatever denomination it may belong, is the deadly enemy of science.

In striving for the attainment of these objects, I have been but one among many, and I shall be well content to be remembered, or even not remembered, as such. Circumstances, among which I am proud to reckon the devoted kindness of many friends, have led to my occupation of various prominent positions, among which the Presidency of the Royal Society is the highest. It would be mock modesty on my part, with these and other scientific honours which have been bestowed upon me, to pretend that I have not suc-ceeded in the career which I have followed, rather because I was driven into it than of my own free will; but I am afraid I should not count even these things as marks of success if I could not hope that I had somewhat helped that movement of opinion which has been called the New Reformation.

ON THE ADVISABLENESS OF IMPROVEING NATURAL KNOWLEDGE

THIS time two hundred years ago — in the beginning of January, 1666 — those of our forefathers who inhabited this great and ancient city, took breath between the shocks of two fearful calamities: one not quite past, although its fury had abated; the other to come.

Within a few yards of the very spot on which we are assembled, so the tradition runs, that painful and deadly malady, the plague, appeared in the latter months of 1664; and, though no new visitor, smote the people of England, and especially of her capital, with a violence unknown before, in the course of the following year. The hand of a master has pictured what happened in those dismal months; and in that truest of fictions, *The History of the Plague Year,* Defoe shows death, with every accompaniment of pain and terror, stalking through the narrow streets of old London, and changing their busy hum into a silence broken only by the wailing of the mourners of fifty thousand dead; by the woful denunciations and mad prayers of fanatics; and by the madder yells of de-spairing profligates.

But, about this time in 1666, the death-rate had sunk to nearly its ordinary amount; a case of plague occurred only here and there, and the richer citizens who had flown from the pest had returned to their dwellings. The remnant of the people began to toil at the accustomed round of duty, or of pleasure; and the stream of city life bid fair to flow back along its old bed, with renewed and uninterrupted vigour.

The newly kindled hope was deceitful. The great plague, indeed, returned no more; but what it had done for the Londoners, the great fire, which broke out in the autumn of 1666, did for London; and, in September of that year, a heap of ashes and the indestructible energy of the people were all that remained of the glory of five-sixths of the city within the walls.

Our forefathers had their own ways of accounting for each of these calamities. They submitted to the plague in humility and in penitence, for they believed it to be the judgment of God. But, towards the fire they were furiously indignant, interpreting it as the effect of the malice of man, — as the work of the Republicans, or of the Papists, according as their prepossessions ran in favour of loyalty or of Puritanism.

It would, I fancy, have fared but ill with one who, standing where I now stand, in what was then a thickly peopled and fashionable part of London, should have broached to our ancestors the doctrine which I now propound to you — that all their hypotheses were alike wrong; that the plague was no more, in their sense, Divine judgment, than the fire was the work of any political, or of any religious sect; but that they were themselves the authors of both plague and fire, and that they must look to themselves to prevent the recurrence of calamities, to all appearance so peculiarly beyond the reach of human control — so evidently the result of the wrath of God, or of the craft and subtlety of an enemy.

And one may picture to one's self how harmoniously the holy cursing of the Puritan of that day would have chimed in with the unholy cursing and the crackling wit of the Rochesters and Sedleys, and with the revilings of the political fanatics, if my imaginary plain dealer had gone on to say that, if the return of such misfortunes were ever rendered impossible, it would not be in virtue of the victory of the faith of Laud, or of that of Milton; and, as little, by the triumph of republicanism, as by that of monarchy. But that the one thing needful for compassing this end was, that the people of England should second the efforts of an insignificant corporation, the establishment of which, a few years before the epoch of the great plague and the great fire, had been as little noticed, as they were conspicuous.

Some twenty years before the outbreak of the plague a few calm and thoughtful students banded themselves together for the purpose, as they phrased it, of " improving natural knowledge." The ends they proposed to attain cannot be stated more clearly than in the words of one of the founders of the organisation: —

" Our business was (precluding matters of theology and state affairs) to discourse and consider of philo-sophical enquiries, and such as related thereunto: — as Physick, Anatomy, Geometry, Astronomy, Navigation, Staticks, Magneticks,

Chymicks, Mechanicks, and Natural Experiments; with the state of these studies and their cultivation at home and abroad. We then discoursed of the circulation of the blood, the valves in the veins, the venae lacteae, the lymphatic vessels, the Copernican hypothesis, the nature of comets and new stars, the satellites of Jupiter, the oval shape (as it then appeared) of Saturn, the spots on the sun and its turning on its own axis, the inequalities and selenography of the moon, the several phases of Venus and Mercury, the improvement of telescopes and grinding of glasses for that purpose, the weight of air, the possibility or impossibility of vacuities and nature's abhorrence thereof, the Torricellian experiment in quicksilver, the descent of heavy bodies and the degree of acceleration therein, with divers other things of like nature, some of which were then but new discoveries, and others not so generally known and embraced as now they are; with other things appertaining to what hath been called the New Philosophy, which from the times of Galileo at Florence, and Sir Francis Bacon (Lord Verulam) in England, hath been much cultivated in Italy, France, Germany, and other parts abroad, as well as with us in England."

The learned Dr. Wallis, writing in 1696, narrates in these words, what happened half a century before, or about 1645. The associates met at Oxford, in the rooms of Dr. Wilkins, who was destined to become a bishop; and subsequently coming together in London, they attracted the notice of the king. And it is a strange evidence of the taste for knowledge which the most obviously worthless of the Stuarts shared with his father and grandfather, that Charles the Second was not content with saying witty things about his philosophers, but did wise things with regard to them. For he not only bestowed upon them such attention as he could spare from his poodles and his mistresses, but, being in his usual state of impecuniosity, begged for them of the Duke of Ormond; and, that step being without effect, gave them Chelsea College, a charter, and a mace: crowning his favours in the best way they could be crowned, by burdening them no further with royal patronage or state interference.

Thus it was that the half-dozen young men, studious of the " New Philosophy,",who met in one another's lodgings in Oxford or in London, in the middle of the seventeenth century, grew in numerical and in real strength, until, in its latter part, the " Royal Society for the Improvement of Natural Knowledge" had already become famous, and had acquired a claim upon the veneration of Englishmen, which it has ever since retained, as the principal focus of scientific activity in our islands, and the chief champion of the cause it was formed to support.

It was by the aid of the Royal Society that Newton published his *Principia*. If all the books in the world, except the *Philosophical Transaction* were destroyed, it is safe to say that the foundations of physical science would remain unshaken, and that the vast intellectual progress of the last two centuries would be largely, though incompletely, recorded. Nor have any signs of halting or of decrepitude manifested themselves in our own times. As in Dr. Wallis's days, so in these, "our business is, precluding theology and state affairs, to discourse and consider of philosophical enquiries." But our "Mathematick" is one which Newton would have to go to school to learn; our " Staticks, Mechanicks, Magneticks, Chymicks, and Natural Experiments" constitute a mass of physical and chemical knowledge, a glimpse at which would compensate Galileo for the doings of a score of inquisitorial cardinals; our "Physick" and "Anatomy" have embraced such infinite varieties of beings, have laid open such new worlds in time and space, have grappled, not unsuccessfully, with such complex problems, that the eyes of Vesalius and of Harvey might be dazzled by the sight of the tree that has grown out of their grain of mustard seed.

The fact is perhaps rather too much, than too little, forced upon one's notice, nowadays, that all this marvellous intellectual growth has a no less wonderful expression in practical life; and that, in this respect, if in no other, the movement symbolised by the progress of the Royal Society stands without a parallel in the history of mankind.

A series of volumes as bulky as the "Transactions of the Royal Society" might possibly be filled with the subtle speculations of the Schoolmen; not improbably, the obtaining a mastery over the products of mediaeval thought might necessitate an even greater expenditure of time and of energy than the acquirement of the " New Philosophy "; but though such work engrossed the best intellects of Europe for a longer time than has elapsed since the great fire, its effects were "writ in water," so far as our social state is concerned.

On the other hand, if the noble first President of the Royal Society could revisit the upper air and once more gladden his eyes with a sight of the familiar mace, he would find himself in the midst of a material civilisation more different from that of his day, than that of the seventeenth was from that of the first century. And if Lord

Brouncker's native sagacity had not deserted his ghost, he would need no long reflection to discover that all these great ships, these railways, these telegraphs, these factories, these printing-presses, without which the whole fabric of modern English society would collapse into a mass of stagnant and starving pauperism, — that all these pillars of our State are but the ripples and the bubbles upon the surface of that great spiritual stream, the springs of which only, he and his fellows were privileged to see; and seeing, to recognise as that which it behoved them above all things to keep pure and undefiled.

It may not be too great a flight of imagination to conceive our noble *revenant* not forgetful of the great troubles of his own day, and anxious to know how often London had been burned down since his time, and how often the plague had carried off its thousands. He would have to learn that, although London contains tenfold the inflammable matter that it did in 1666; though, not content with filling our rooms with woodwork and light draperies, we must needs lead inflammable and explosive gases into every corner of our streets and houses, we never allow even a street to burn down. And if he asked how this had come about, we should have to explain that the improvement of natural knowledge has furnished us with dozens of machines for throwing water upon fires, any one of which would have furnished the ingenious Mr. Hooke, the first "curator and experimenter" of the Royal Society,with ample materials for discourse before half a dozen meetings of that body; and that, to say truth, except for the progress of natural knowledge, we should not have been able to make even the tools by which these machines are constructed. And, further, it would be necessary to add, that although severe fires sometimes occur and inflict great damage, the loss is very generally compensated by societies, the operations of which have been rendered possible only by the progress of natural knowledge in the direction of mathematics, and the accumulation of wealth in virtue of other natural knowledge.

But the plague ? My Lord Brouncker's observation would not, I fear, lead him to think that Englishmen of the nineteenth century are purer in life, or more fervent in religious faith, than the generation which could produce a Boyle, an Evelyn, and a Milton. He might find the mud of society at the bottom, instead of at the top, but I fear that the sum total would be as deserving of swift judgment as at the time of the Restoration. And it would be our duty to explain once more, and this time not without shame, that we have no reason to believe that it is the improvement of our faith, nor that of our morals, which keeps the plague from our city; but, again, that it is the improvement of our natural knowledge.

We have learned that pestilences will only take up their abode among those who have prepared un-swept and ungarnished residences for them. Their cities must have narrow, unwatered streets, foul with accumulated garbage. Their houses must be ill-drained, ill-lighted, ill-ventilated. Their subjects must be ill-washed, ill-fed, ill-clothed. The London of 1665 was such a city. The cities of the East, where plague has an enduring dwelling, are such cities. We, in later times, have learned somewhat of Nature, and partly obey her. Because of this partial improvement of our natural knowledge and of that fractional obedience, we have no plague; because that knowledge is still very imperfect and that obedience yet incomplete, typhoid is our companion and cholera our visitor. But it is not presumptuous to express the belief that, when our knowledge is more complete and our obedience the expression of our knowledge, London will count her centuries of freedom from typhoid and cholera, as she now gratefully reckons her two hundred years of ignorance of that plague which swooped upon her thrice in the first half of the seventeenth century.

Surely, there is nothing in these explanations which is not fully borne out by the facts ? Surely, the principles involved in them are now admitted among the fixed beliefs of all thinking men ? Surely, it is true that our countrymen are less subject to fire, famine, pestilence, and all the evils which result from a want of command over and due anticipation of the course of Nature, than were the countrymen of Milton; and health, wealth, and well-being are more abundant with us than with them ? But no less certainly is the difference due to the improvement of our knowledge of Nature, and the extent to which that improved knowledge has been incorporated with the household words of men, and has supplied the springs of their daily actions.

Granting for a moment, then, the truth of that which the depredators of natural knowledge are so fond of urging, that its improvement can only add to the resources of our material civilisation; admitting it to be possible that the founders of the Royal Society themselves looked for not other reward than this, I cannot confess that I was guilty of exaggeration when I hinted, that to him who had the gift of distinguishing between prominent events and important events, the origin of a combined effort on the part of mankind to improve natural knowledge might have loomed larger than the Plague and have outshone the glare of the Fire; as a something fraught with a wealth of beneficence to mankind, in comparison with which the damage done by those ghastly evils would shrink into insignificance.

It is very certain that for every victim slain by the plague, hundreds of mankind exist and find a fair share of happiness in the world by the aid of the spinning jenny. And the great fire, at its worst, could not have burned the supply of coal, the daily working of which, in the bowels of the earth, made possible by the steam pump, gives rise to an amount of wealth to which the millions lost in old London are but as an old song.

But spinning jenny and steam pump are, after all, but toys, possessing an accidental value; and natural knowledge creates multitudes of more subtle contrivances, the praises of which do not happen to be sung because they are not directly convertible into instruments for creating wealth. When I contemplate natural knowledge squandering such gifts among men, the only appropriate comparison I can find for her is to liken her to such a peasant woman as one sees in the Alps, striding ever upward, heavily burdened, and with mind bent only on her home; but yet without effort and without thought, knitting for her children. Now stockings are good and comfortable things, and the children will undoubtedly be much the better for them; but surely it would be short-sighted, to say the least of it, to depreciate this toiling mother as a mere stocking-machine — a mere provider of physical comforts ?

However, there are blind leaders of the blind, and not a few of them, who take this view of natural knowledge, and can see nothing in the bountiful mother of humanity but a sort of comfort-grinding machine. According to them, the improvement of natural knowledge always has been, and always must be, synonymous with no more than the improvement of the material resources and the increase of the gratifications of men.

Natural knowledge is, in their eyes, no real mother of mankind, bringing them up with kindness, and, if need be, with sternness, in the way they should go, and instructing them in all things needful for their welfare; but a sort of fairy god-mother, ready to furnish her pets with shoes of swiftness, swords of sharpness, and omnipotent Aladdin's lamps, so that they may have telegraphs to Saturn, and see the other side of the moon, and thank God they are better than their benighted ancestors.

If this talk were true, I, for one, should not greatly care to toil in the service of natural knowledge. I think I would just as soon be quietly chipping my own flint axe, after the manner of my forefathers a few thousand years back, as be troubled with the endless malady of thought which now infests us all, for such reward. But I venture to say that such views are contrary alike to reason and to fact. Those who discourse in such fashion seem to me to be so intent upon trying to see what is above Nature, or what is behind her, that they are blind to what stares them in the face in her.

I should not venture thus to speak strongly if my jus-tification were not to be found in the simplest and most obvious facts, — if it needed more than an appeal to the most notorious truths to justify my assertion, that the improvement of natural knowledge, whatever direction it has taken, and however low the aims of those who may have commenced it — has not only conferred practical benefits on men, but, in so doing, has effected a revolution in their conceptions of the universe and of themselves, and has profoundly altered their modes of thinking and their views of right and wrong. I say that natural knowledge, seeking to satisfy natural wants, has found the ideas which can alone still spiritual cravings. I say that natural knowl-edge, in desiring to ascertain the laws of comfort, has been driven to discover those of conduct, and to lay the foundations of a new morality.

Let us take these points separately; and first, what great ideas has natural knowl-edge introduced into men's minds ?

I cannot but think that the foundations of all natural knowledge were laid when the reason of man first came face to face with the facts of Nature; when the savage first learned that the fingers of one hand are fewer than those of both; that it is shorter to cross a stream than to head it; that a stone stops where it is unless it be moved, and that it drops from the hand which lets it go; that light and heat come and go with the sun; that sticks burn away in a fire; that plants and animals grow and die; that if he struck his fellow savage a blow he would make him angry, and perhaps get a blow in return, while if he offered him a fruit he would please him, and perhaps receive a fish in exchange. When men had acquired this much knowl-edge, the outlines, rude though they were, of mathematics, of physics, of chemistry, of biology, of moral, economical, and political science, were sketched. Nor did the germ of religion fail when science began to bud. Listen to words which, though new, are yet three thousand years old: —

. . . When in heaven the stars about the moon Look beautiful, when all the winds are laid, And every height comes out, and jutting peak And valley, and the immeasurable heavens Break open to their highest, and all the stars Shine, and the shepherd gladdens in his heart

If the half savage Greek could share our feelings thus far, it is irrational to doubt that he went further, to find as we do, that upon that brief gladness there follows a certain sorrow, — the little light of awakened human intelligence shines so mere a spark amidst the abyss of the unknown and unknowable; seems so insufficient to do more than illuminate the imperfections that cannot be remedied, the aspirations that cannot be realised, of man's own nature. But in this sadness, this consciousness of the limitation of man, this sense of an open secret which he cannot penetrate, lies the essence of all religion; and the attempt to embody it in the forms furnished by the intellect is the origin of the higher theologies.

Thus it seems impossible to imagine but that the foundations of all knowledge — secular or sacred — were laid when intelligence dawned, though the super-structure remained for long ages so slight and feeble as to be compatible with the existence of almost any general view respecting the mode of governance of the universe. No doubt, from the first, there were certain phaenomena which, to the rudest mind, presented a constancy of occurrence, and suggested that a fixed order ruled, at any rate, among them. I doubt if the grossest of Fetish worshippers ever imagined that a stone must have a god within it to make it fall, or that a fruit had a god within it to make it taste sweet. With regard to such matters as these, it is hardly question-able that mankind from the first took strictly positive and scientific views.

But, with respect to all the less familiar occurrences which present themselves, uncultured man, no doubt, has always taken himself as the standard of comparison, as the centre and measure of the world; nor could he well avoid doing so. And find-ing that his apparently uncaused will has a powerful effect in giving rise to many occurrences, he naturally enough ascribed other and greater events to other and greater volitions, and came to look upon the world and all that therein is, as the product of the volitions of persons like himself, but stronger, and capable of being appeased or angered, as he himself might be soothed or irritated. Through such conceptions of the plan and working of the universe all mankind have passed, or are passing. And we may now consider what has been the effect of the improvement of natural knowledge on the views of men who have reached this stage, and who have begun to cultivate natural knowledge with no desire but that of "increasing God's honour and bettering man's estate."

For example, what could seem wiser, from a mere material point of view, more innocent, from a theological one, to an ancient people, than that they should learn the exact succession of the seasons, as warnings for their husbandmen; or the position of the stars, as guides to their rude navigators ? But what has grown out of this search for natural knowledge of so merely useful a character ? You all know the reply. Astronomy, — which of all sciences has filled men's minds with general ideas of a character most foreign to their daily experience, and has, more than any other, rendered it impossible for them to accept the beliefs of their fathers. Astronomy, — which tells them that this so vast and seemingly solid earth is but an atom among atoms, whirling, no man knows whither, through illimitable space; which demonstrates that what we call the peaceful heaven above us, is but that space, filled by an infinitely subtle matter whose particles are seething and surging, like the waves of an angry sea; which opens up to us infinite regions where nothing is known, or ever seems to have been known, but matter and force, operating according to rigid rules; which leads us to contemplate phaenomena the very nature of which demonstrates that they must have had a beginning, and that they must have an end, but the very nature of which also proves that the beginning was, to our conceptions of time, infinitely remote, and that the end is as immeasurably distant.

But it is not alone those who pursue astronomy who ask for bread and receive ideas. What more harmless than the attempt to lift and distribute water by pumping it; what more absolutely and grossly utilitarian? Yet out of pumps grew the discussions about Nature's abhorrence of a vacuum; and then it was discovered that Nature does not abhor a vacuum, but that air has weight; and that notion paved the way for the doctrine that all matter has weight, and that the force which produces weight is co-extensive with the universe, — in short, to the theory of universal gravitation and endless force. While learning how to handle gases led to the discovery of oxygen, and to modern chemistry, and to the notion of the indestructibility of matter.

Again, what simpler, or more absolutely practical, than the attempt to keep the axle of a wheel from heating when the wheel turns round very fast? How useful for carters and gig drivers to know something about this; and how good were it, if any ingenious person would find out the cause of such phaenomena, and thence educe a general remedy for them. Such an ingenious person was Count Rumford; and he and his successors have landed us in the theory of the persistence, or indestructibility, of force. And in the infinitely minute, as in the infinitely great, the seekers after natural knowledge of the kinds called physical and chemical, have everywhere found a definite order and succession of events which seem never to be in-fringed.

And how has it fared with "Physick" and Anat-omy? Have the anatomist, the physiologist, or the physician, whose business it has been to devote themselves assiduously to that eminently practical and direct end, the alleviation of the sufferings of mankind, — have they been able to confine their vision more absolutely to the strictly useful? I fear they are the worst offenders of all. For if the astronomer has-set before us the infinite magnitude of space, and the practical eternity of the duration of the universe; if the physical and chemical philosophers have demonstrated the infinite minuteness of its constituent parts, and the practical eternity of matter and of force; and if both have alike proclaimed the universality of a definite and predicable order and succession of events, the workers in biology have not only accepted all these, but have added more startling theses of their own. For, as the astronomers discover in the earth no centre of the universe, but an eccentric speck, so the naturalists find man to be no centre of the living world, but one amidst endless modifications of life; and as the astronomers observe the mark of practically endless time set upon the arrangements of the solar system so the student of life finds the records of ancient' forms of existence peopling the world for ages, which, in relation to human experience, are infinite.

Furthermore, the physiologist finds life to be as dependent for its manifestation of particular molecular arrangements as any physical or chemical phenomenon; and wherever he extends his researches, fixed order and unchanging causation reveal themselves, as plainly as in the rest of Nature.

Nor can I find that any other fate has awaited the germ of Religion. Arising, like all other kinds of knowledge, out of the action and interaction of man's mind, with that which is not man's mind, it has taken the intellectual coverings of Fetishism or Polytheism; of Theism or Atheism; of Superstition or Rationalism. With these, and their relative merits and demerits, I have nothing to do; but this it is needful for my purpose to say, that if the religion of the present differs from that of the past, it is because the theology of the present has become more scientific than that of the past; because it has not only renounced idols of wood and idols of stone, but begins to see the necessity of breaking in pieces the idols built up of books and traditions and fine-spun ecclesiastical cobwebs: and of cherishing the noblest and most human of man's emotions, by worship "for the most part of the silent sort" at the Altar of the Unknown.

Such are a few of the new conceptions implanted in our minds by the improvement of natural knowledge. Men have acquired the ideas of the practically infinite extent of the universe and of its practical eternity; they are familiar with the conception that our earth is but an infinitesimal fragment of that part of the universe which can be seen; and that, nevertheless, its duration is, as compared with our standards of time, infinite. They have further acquired the idea that man is but one of innumerable forms of life now existing on the globe, and that the present existences are but the last of an immeasurable series of predecessors. Moreover, every step they have made in natural knowledge has tended to extend and rivet in their minds the conception of a definite order of the universe — which is embodied in what are called, by an unhappy metaphor, the laws of Nature — and to narrow the range and loosen the force of men's belief in spontaneity, or in changes other than such as arise out of that definite order itself.

Whether these ideas are well or ill founded is not the question. No one can deny that they exist, and have been the inevitable outgrowth of the improvement of natural knowledge. And if so, it cannot be doubted that they are changing the form of men's most cherished and most important convictions.

And as regards the second point — the extent to which the improvement of natural knowledge has remodelled and altered what may be termed the intellectual ethics of men, —what are among the moral convictions most fondly held by barbarous and semi-barbarous people ?

They are the convictions that authority is the soundest basis of belief; that merit attaches to a readiness to believe; that the doubting disposition is a bad one, and scepticism a sin; that when good authority has pronounced what is to be believed, and faith has accepted it, reason has no further duty. There are many excellent persons who yet hold by these principles, and it is not my present business, or intention, to discuss their views. All I wish to bring clearly before your minds is the unquestionable fact, that the improvement of natural knowledge is effected by methods which directly give the lie to all these convictions, and assume the exact reverse of each to be true.

The improver of natural knowledge absolutely refuses to acknowledge authority, as such. For him, scepticism is the highest of duties; blind faith the one unpardonable sin. And it cannot be otherwise, for every great advance in natural knowledge has involved the absolute rejection of authority, the cherishing of the keenest scepticism, the annihilation of the spirit of blind faith; and the most ardent votary of science holds his firmest convictions, not because the men he most venerates hold them; not because their verity is testified by portents and wonders; but because his experience teaches him that whenever he chooses to bring these convictions into contact with their primary source, Nature — whenever he thinks fit to test them by appealing to experiment and to observation — Nature will confirm them. The man of science has learned to believe in justification, not by faith, but by verification.

Thus, without for a moment pretending to despise the practical results of the improvement of natural knowledge, and its beneficial influence on material civilisation, it must, I think, be admitted that the great ideas, some of which I have indicated, and the ethical spirit which I have endeavoured to sketch, in the few moments which remained at my disposal, constitute the real and permanent significance of natural knowledge.

If these ideas be destined, as I believe they are, to be more and more firmly established as the world grows older; if that spirit be fated, as I believe it is, to extend itself into all departments of human thought, and to become co-extensive with the range of knowledge; if, as our race approaches its maturity, it discovers, as I believe it will, that there is but one kind of knowledge and but one method of acquiring it; then we, who are still children, may justly feel it our highest duty to recognise the advisableness of improving natural knowledge, and so to aid ourselves and our successors in our course towards the noble goal which lies before mankind.

A LIBERAL EDUCATION

THE business which the South London Working Men's College has undertaken is a great work; indeed, I might say, that Education, with which that college proposes to grapple, is the greatest work of all those which lie ready to a man's hand just at present.

And, at length, this fact is becoming generally recognised. You cannot go anywhere without hearing a buzz of more or less confused and contradictory talk on this subject — nor can you fail to notice that, in one point at any rate, there is a very decided advance upon like discussions in former days. Nobody outside the agricultural interest now dares to say that education is a bad thing. If any representative of the once large and powerful party, which, in former days, proclaimed this opinion, still exists in the semi-fossil state, he keeps his thoughts to himself. In fact, there is a chorus of voices, almost distressing in their harmony, raised in favour of the doctrine that education is the great panacea for human troubles, and that, if the country is not shortly to go to the dogs, everybody must be educated.

The politicians tell us, "You must educate the masses because they are going to be masters." The clergy join in the cry for education, for they affirm that the people are drifting away from church and chapel into the broadest infidelity. The manufacturers and the capitalists swell the chorus lustily. They declare that ignorance makes bad workmen; that England will soon be unable to turn out cotton goods, or steam enginest cheaper than other people; and then, Ichabod! Ichabod! the glory will be departed from us. And a few voices are lifted up in favour of the doctrine that the masses should be educated because they are men and women with unlimited capacities of being, doing, and suffering, and that it is as true now, as it ever was, that the people perish for lack of knowledge.

These members of the minority, with whom I confess I have a good deal of sympathy, are doubtful whether any of the other reasons urged in favour of the education of the people are of much value — whether, indeed, some of them are based upon either wise or noble grounds of action. They question if it be wise to tell people that you will do for them, out of fear of their power, what you have left undone, so long as your only motive was compassion for their weakness and their sorrows. And, if ignorance of everything which is needful a ruler should know is likely to do so much harm in the governing classes of the future, why is it, they ask reasonably enough, that such ignorance in the governing classes of the past has not been viewed with equal horror ?

Compare the average artisan and the average country squire, and it may be doubted if you will find a pin to choose between the two in point of ignorance, class feeling, or prejudice. It is true that the ignorance is of a different sort — that the class feeling is in favour of a different class — and that the prejudice has a distinct savour of wrong-headedness in each case — but it is questionable if the one is either a bit better, or a bit worse, than the other. The old protectionist theory is the doctrine of trades unions as applied by the squires, and the modern trades unionism is the doctrine of the squires applied by the artisans. Why should we be worse off under one régime than under the other?

Again, this sceptical minority asks the clergy to think whether it is really want of education which keeps the masses away from their ministrations — whether the most completely educated men are not as open to reproach on this score as the workmen; and whether, perchance, this may not indicate that it is not education which lies at the bottom of the matter ?

Once more, these people, whom there is no pleasing, venture to doubt whether the glory which rests upon being able to undersell all the rest of the world, is a very safe kind of glory — whether we may not purchase it too dear; especially if we allow education, which ought to be directed to the making of men, to be diverted into a process of manufacturing human tools, wonderfully adroit in the exercise of some technical industry, but good for nothing else.

And, finally, these people inquire whether it is the masses alone who need a reformed and improved education. They ask whether the richest of our public schools might not well be made to supply knowledge, as well as gentlemanly habits, a strong class feeling, and eminent proficiency in cricket. They seem to think that the noble foundations of our old universities are hardly fulfilling their functions in their present posture of half-clerical Seminaries, half racecourses, where men are trained to win a senior wranglership, or a double-first, as horses are trained to win a cup, with as little reference to the needs of after-life in the case of a man as in that of the racer. And, while as zealous for education as the rest, they affirm that, if the education of the richer classes were such as to fit them to be the leaders and the governors of the poorer; and, if the education of the poorer classes were such as to enable them to appreciate really wise guidance and good governance, the politicians need not fear mob-law, nor the clergy lament their want of flocks, nor the capitalists prognosticate the annihilation of the prosperity of the country.

Such is the diversity of opinion upon the why and the wherefore of education. And my hearers will be prepared to expect that the practical recommendations which are put forward are not less discordant. There is a loud cry for compulsory education. We English, in spite of constant experience to the contrary, preserve a touching faith in the efficacy of acts of Parliament; and I believe we should have compulsory education in the courses of next session, if there were the least probability that half a dozen leading statesmen of different parties would agree what that education should be.

Some hold that education without theology is worse than none. Others maintain, quite as strongly, that education with theology is in the same predicament. But this is certain, that those who hold the first opinion can by no means agree what theology should be taught; and that those who maintain the second are in a small minority.

At any rate "make people learn to read, write, and cipher," say a great many; arid the advice is undoubtedly sensible as far as it goes. But, as has happened to me in former days, those who, in despair of getting anything better, advocate this measure, are met with the objection that it is very like making a child practise the use of a knife, fork, and spoon, without giving it a particle of meat. I really don't know what reply is to be made to such an objection.

But it would be unprofitable to spend more time in disentangling, or rather in showing up the knots in, the ravelled skeins of our neighbours. Much more to the purpose is it to ask if we possess any clue of our own which may guide us among these entanglements. And by way of a beginning, let us ask ourselves — What is education? Above all things, what is our ideal of a thoroughly liberal education? — of that education which, if we could begin life again, we would give ourselves — of that education which, if we could mould the fates to our own will, we would give our children? Well, I know not what may be your conceptions upon this matter, but I will tell you mine, and I hope I shall find that our views are not very discrepant.

Suppose it were perfectly certain that the life and fortune of every one of us would, one day or other, depend upon his winning or losing a game of chess. Don't you think that we should all consider it to be a primary duty to learn at least the names and the moves of the pieces; to have a notion of a gambit, and a keen eye for all the means of giving and getting out of check ? Do you not think that we should look with a disapprobation amounting to scorn, upon the father who allowed his son, or the state which allowed its members, to grow up without knowing a pawn from a knight ?

Yet it is a very plain and elementary truth, that the life, the fortune, and the happiness of every one of us, and, more or less, of those who are connected with us, do depend upon our knowing something of the rules of a game infinitely more difficult and complicated than chess. It is a game which has been played for untold ages, every man and woman of us being one of the two players in a game of his or her own. The chessboard is the world, the pieces are the phenomena of the universe, the rules of the game are what we call the laws of Nature. The player on the other side is hidden from us. We know that his play is always fair, just, and patient. But also we know, to our cost, that he never overlooks a mistake, or makes the smallest allowance for ignorance. To the man who plays well, the highest stakes are paid, with that sort of overflowing generosity with which the strong shows delight in strength. And one who plays ill is checkmated — without haste, but without remorse.

My metaphor will remind some of you of the famous picture in which Retzsch has depicted Satan playing at chess with man for his soul. Substitute for the mocking fiend in that picture a calm, strong angel who is playing for love, as we say, and would rather lose than win — and I should accept it as an image of human life.

Well, what I mean by Education is learning the rules of this mighty game. In other words, education is the instruction of the intellect in the laws of Nature, under which name I include not merely things and their forces, but men and their ways; and the fashioning of the affections and of the will into an earnest and loving desire to move in harmony with those laws. For me, education means neither more nor less than this. Anything which professes to call itself education must be tried by this standard, and if it fails to stand the test, I will not call it education, whatever may be the force of authority, or of numbers, upon the other side.

It is important to remember that, in strictness, there is no such thing as an un-educated man. Take an extreme case. Suppose that an adult man, in the full vigour of his faculties, could be suddenly placed in the world, as Adam is said to have been, and then left to do as he best might. How long would he be left uneducated ? Not five minutes. Nature would begin to teach him, through the eye, the ear, the touch, the properties of objects. Pain and pleasure would be at his elbow telling him to do this and avoid that; and by slow degrees the man would receive an education which, if narrow, would be thorough, real, and adequate to his circumstances, though there would be no extras and very few accomplishments.

And if to this solitary man entered a second Adam or, better still, an Eve, a new and greater world, that of social and moral phenomena, would be revealed. Joys and woes, compared with which all others might seem but faint shadows, would spring from the new relations. Happiness and sorrow would take the place of the coarser monitors, pleasure and pain; but conduct would still be shaped by the observation of the natural consequences of actions; or, in other words, by the laws of the nature of man.

To every one of us the world was once as fresh and new as to Adam. And then, long before we were susceptible of any other modes of instruction, Nature took us in hand, and every minute of waking life brought its educational influence, shaping our actions into rough accordance with Nature's laws, so that we might not be ended untimely by too gross disobedience. Nor should I speak of this process of education as past for any one, be he as old as he may. For every man the world is as fresh as it was at the first day, and as full of untold novelties for him who has the eyes to see them. And Nature is still continuing her patient education of us in that great university, the universe, of which we are all members — Nature having no Test-Acts.

Those who take honours in Nature's university, who learn the laws which govern men and things and obey them, are the really great and successful men in this world. The great mass of mankind are the " Poll," who pick up just enough to get through without much discredit. Those who won't learn at all are plucked; and then you can't come up again. Nature's pluck means extermination.

Thus the question of compulsory education is settled so far as Nature is concerned. Her bill on that question was framed and passed long ago. But like all compulsory legislation, that of Nature is harsh and wasteful in its operation. Ignorance is visited as sharply as wilful disobedience — incapacity meets with the same punishment as crime. Nature's discipline is not even a word and a blow, and the blow first; but the blow without the word. It is left to you to find out why your ears are boxed.

The object of what we commonly call education — that education in which man intervenes and which I shall distinguish as artificial education — is to make good these defects in Nature's methods; to prepare the child to receive Nature's education, neither incapably nor ignorantly, nor with wilful disobedience; and to understand the preliminary symptoms of her pleasure, without waiting for the box on the ear. In short, all artificial education ought to be an anticipation of natural education. And a liberal education is an artificial education which has not only prepared a man to escape the great evils of disobedience to natural laws, but has trained him to appreciate and to seize upon the rewards, which Nature scatters with as free a hand as her penalties.

That man, I think, has had a liberal education who has been so trained in youth that his body is the ready servant of his will, and does with ease and pleasure all the work that, as a mechanism, it is capable of; whose intellect is a clear, cold, logic engine, with all its parts of equal strength, and in smooth working order; ready, like a steam engine, to be turned to any kind of work, and spin the gossamers as well as forge the anchors of the mind; whose mind is stored with a knowledge of the great and fundamental truths of Nature and of the laws of her operations; one who, no stunted ascetic, is full of life and fire, but whose passions are trained to come to heel by a vigorous will, the servant of a tender conscience; who has learned to love all beauty, whether of Nature or of art, to hate all vileness, and to respect others as himself.

Such an one and no other, I conceive, has had a liberal education; for he is, as completely as a man can be, in harmony with Nature. He will make the best of her, and she of him. They will get on together rarely; she as his ever beneficent mother; he as her mouthpiece, her conscious self, her minister and interpreter.

ON A PIECE OF CHALK

IF a well were sunk at our feet in the midst of the city of Norwich, the diggers would very soon find themselves at work in that white substance almost too soft to be called rock, with which we are all familiar as "chalk."

Not only here, but over the whole county of Norfolk, the well-sinker might carry his shaft down many hundred feet without coming to the end of the chalk; and, on the sea-coast, where the waves have pared away the face of the land which breasts them, the scarped faces of the high cliffs are often wholly formed of the same material. Northward, the chalk may be followed as far as Yorkshire; on the south coast it appears abruptly in the picturesque western bays of Dorset, and breaks into the Needles of the Isle of Wight; while on the shores of Kent it supplies that long line of white cliffs to which England owes her name of Albion.

Were the thin soil which covers it all washed away, a curved band of white chalk, here broader, and there narrower, might be followed diagonally across England from Lulworth in Dorset, to Flamborough Head in Yorkshire — a distance of over two hundred and eighty miles as the crow flies.

From this band to the North Sea, on the east, and the Channel, on the South, the chalk is largely hidden by other deposits; but, except in the Weald of Kent and Sussex, it enters into the very foundation of all the south-eastern counties.

Attaining, as it does in some places, a thickness of more than a thousand feet, the English chalk must be admitted to be a mass of considerable magnitude. Nevertheless, it covers but an insignificant portion of the whole area occupied by the chalk formation of the globe, which has precisely the same general characters as ours, and is found in detached patches, some less, and others more extensive, than the English.

Chalk occurs in north-west Ireland; it stretches over a large part of France, — the chalk which underlies Paris being, in fact, a continuation of that of the London basin; it runs through Denmark and Central Europe, and extends southward to North Africa; while eastward, it appears in the Crimea and in Syria, and may be traced as far as the shores of the Sea of Aral, in Central Asia.

If all the points at which true chalk occurs were circumscribed, they would lie within an irregular oval about three thousand miles in long diameter — the area of which would be as great as that of Europe, and would many times exceed that of the largest existing inland sea — the Mediterranean.

Thus the chalk is no unimportant element in the masonry of the earth's crust, and it impresses a peculiar stamp, varying with the conditions to which it is exposed, on the scenery of the districts in which it occurs. The undulating downs and rounded coombs, covered with sweet-grassed turf, of our inland chalk country, have a peacefully domestic and mutton-suggesting prettiness, but can hardly be called either grand or beautiful. But on our southern coasts, the wall-sided cliffs, many hundred feet high, with vast necdles and pinnacles standing out in the sea, sharp and solitary enough to serve as perches for the wary cormorant, confer a wonderful beauty and grandeur upon the chalk headlands. And, in the East, chalk has its share in the formation of some of the most venerable of mountain ranges, such as the Lebanon.

What is this wide-spread component of the surface of the earth ? and whence did it come ?

You may think this no very hopeful inquiry. You may not unnaturally suppose that the attempt to solve such problems as these can lead to no result, save that of entangling the inquirer in vague speculations, incapable of refutation and of verification.

If such were really the case, I should have selected some other subject than a "piece of chalk" for my discourse. But, in truth, after much deliberation, I have been unable to think of any topic which would so well enable me to lead you to see how solid is the foundation upon which some of the most startling conclusions of physical science rest.

A great chapter of the history of the world is written in the chalk. Few passages in the history of man can be supported by such an overwhelming mass of direct and indirect evidence as that which testifies to the truth of the fragment of the history of the globe, which I hope to enable you to read, with your own eyes, tonight.

Let me add, that few chapters of human history have a more profound significance for ourselves. I weigh my words well when I assert, that the man who should know the true history of the bit of chalk which every carpenter carries about in his breeches-pocket, though ignorant of all other history, is likely, if he will think his knowledge out to its ultimate results, to have a truer, and therefore a better, conception of this wonderful universe, and of man's relation to it, than the most learned student who is deep-read in the records of humanity and ignorant of those of Nature.

The language of the chalk is not hard to learn, not nearly so hard as Latin, if you only want to get at the broad features of the story it has to tell; and I propose that we now set to work to spell that story out together.

We all know that if we " burn" chalk the result is quicklime. Chalk, in fact, is a compound of carbonic acid gas, and lime, and when you make it very hot the carbonic acid flies away and the lime is left.

By this method of procedure we see the lime, but we do not see the carbonic acid. If, on the other hand, you were to powder a little chalk and drop it into a good deal of strong vinegar, there would be a great bubbling and fizzing, and, finally, a clear liquid, in which no sign of chalk would appear. Here you see the carbonic acid in the bubbles; the lime, dissolved in the vinegar, vanishes from sight. There are a great many other ways of showing that chalk is essentially nothing but carbonic acid and quicklime. Chemists enunciate the result of all the experiments which prove this, by stating that chalk is almost wholly com-posed of "carbonate of lime."

It is desirable for us to start from the knowledge of this fact, though it may not seem to help us very far towards what we seek. For carbonate of lime is a widely spread substance, and is met with under very various conditions. All sorts of lime-stones are composed of more or less pure carbonate of lime. The crust which is often deposited by waters which have drained through limestone rocks, in the form of what are called stalagmites and stalactites, is carbonate of lime. Or, to take a more familiar example, the fur on the inside of a tea-kettle is carbonate of lime; and, for anything chemistry tells us to the contrary, the chalk might be a kind of gigantic fur upon the bottom of the earth-kettle, which is kept pretty hot below.

Let us try another method of making the chalk tell us its own history. To the unassisted eye chalk looks simply like a very loose and open kind of stone. But it is possible to grind a slice of chalk down so thin that you can see through it — until it is thin enough, in fact, to be examined with any magnifying power that may be thought desirable. A thin slice of the fur of a kettle might be made in the same way.

If it were examined microscopically, it would show itself to be a more or less distinctly laminated mineral substance and nothing more.

But the slice of chalk presents a totally different appearance when placed under the microscope. The general mass of it is made up of very minute granules; but, imbedded in this matrix, are innumerable bodies, some smaller and some larger, but, on a rough average, not more than a hundredth of an inch in diameter, having a well-defined shape and structure. A cubic inch of some specimens of chalk may contain hundreds of thousands of these bodies, compacted together with incalculable millions of the granules.

The examination of a transparent slice gives a good notion of the manner in which the components of the chalk are arranged, and of their relative proportions. But, by rubbing up some chalk with a brush in water and then pouring off the milky fluid, so as to obtain sediments of different degrees of fineness, the granules and the minute rounded bodies may be pretty well separated from one another, and submitted to microscopic examination, either as opaque or as transparent objects. By combining the views obtained in these various methods, each of the rounded bodies may be proved to be a beautifully constructed calcareous fabric, made up of a number of chambers, communicating freely with one another. The chambered bodies are of various forms. One of the commonest is something like a badly grown raspberry, being formed of a number of nearly globular chambers of different sizes congregated together. It is called *Globigerina, and some specimens of chalk consist of little else than Globigerince* and granules.

Let us fix our attention upon the *Globigerina*. It is the spoor of the game we are tracking. If we can learn what it is and what are the conditions of its existence, we shall see our way to the origin and past history of the chalk.

A suggestion which may naturally enough present itself is, that these curious bodies are the result of some process of aggregation which has taken place in the carbonate of lime; that, just as in winter, the rime on our windows simulates the most delicate and elegantly arborescent foliage — proving that the mere mineral water may, under certain conditions, assume the outward form of organic bodies — so this mineral substance, carbonate of lime, hidden away in the bowels -of the earth, has taken the shape of these chambered bodies. I am not raising a merely fanciful and unreal objection. Very learned men, in former days, have even enter-tained the notion that all the formed things found in rocks are of this nature; and if no such conception is at present ,held to be admissible, it is because long and varied experience has now shown that mineral matter never does assume the form and structure we find in fossils. If any one were to try to per* suade you that an oyster-shell (which is also chiefly composed of carbonate of lime) had crystallized out of sea-water, I suppose you would laugh at the absurdity. Your laughter would be justified by the fact that all experience tends to show that oyster-shells are formed by the agency of oysters, and in no other way. And if there were no better reasons, we should be justified, on like grounds, in believing that *Globigerina* is not the product of anything but vital activity.

Happily, however, better evidence in proof of the organic nature of the *Globtgerince* than that of analogy is forthcoming. It so happens that calcareous skeletons, exactly similar to the *Globigerince* of the chalk, are being formed, at the present moment, by minute living creatures, which flourish in multitudes, literally more numerous than the sands of the sea-shore, over a large extent of that part of the earth's surface which is covered by the ocean.

The history of the discovery of these living *Globigerince*, and of the part which they play in rock building, is singular enough. It is a discovery which, like others of no less scientific importance, has arisen, in-cidentally, out of work devoted to very different and exceedingly practical interests.

When men first took to the sea, they speedily learned to look out for shoals and rocks; and the more the burthen of their ships increased, the more imperatively necessary it became for sailors to ascertain with precision the depths of the waters they traversed. Out of this necessity grew the use of the lead and sounding line; and, ultimately, marine-surveying, which is the recording of the form of coasts and of the depth of the sea, as ascertained by the sounding-lead, upon charts.

At the same time, it became desirable to ascertain and to indicate the nature of the sea-bottom, since this circumstance greatly affects its goodness as holding ground for anchors. Some ingenious tar, whose name deserves a better fate than the oblivion into which it has fallen, attained this object by "arming" the bottom of the lead with a lump of grease, to which more or less of the sand or mud, or broken shells, as the case might be, adhered, and was brought to the surface. But, however well adapted such an apparatus might be for rough nautical purposes, scientific accuracy could not be expected from the armed lead, and to remedy its defects (especially when applied to sounding in great depths) Lieut. Brooke, of the American Navy, some years ago invented a most ingenious machine, by which a considerable portion of the superficial layer of the sea-bottom can be scooped out and brought up from any depth to which the lead descends.

In 1853, Lieut. Brooke obtained mud from the bottom of the North Atlantic, between Newfoundland and the Azores, at a depth of more than ten thousand feet, or two miles, by the help of this sounding apparatus. The specimens were sent for examination to Ehrenberg of Berlin, and to Bailey of West Point, and those able microscopists found that this deep-sea mud was almost entirely composed of the skeletons of living organisms — the greater proportion of these being just like the *Globigerince* already known to occur in the chalk.

Thus far, the work had been carried on simply in the interests of science, but Lieut. Brooke's method of sounding acquired a high commercial value, when the enterprise of laying down the telegraph-cable between this country and the United States was undertaken. For it became a matter of immense importance to know, not only the depth of the sea over the whole line along which the cable was to be laid, but the exact nature of the bottom, so as to guard against chances of cutting or fraying the strands of that costly rope. The Admiralty consequently ordered Captain Dayman, an old friend and shipmate of mine, to ascertain the depth over the whole line of the cable, and to bring back specimens of the bottom. In former days, such a command as this might have sounded very much like one of the impossible things which the young prince in the Fairy Tales is ordered to do before he can obtain the hand of the Princess. However, in the months of June and July, 1857, my friend performed the task assigned to him with great expedition and precision without, so far as I know, having met with any reward of that kind. The specimens of Atlantic mud which he procured were sent to me to be examined and reported upon[1].

The result of all these operations is, that we know the contours and the nature of the surface-soil covered by the North Atlantic, for a distance of seventeen hun-

---

1   See Appendix to Captain Dayman's " Deep-sea Soundings in the North Atlantic Ocean, between Ireland and Newfoundland, made in H.M.S. Cyclops. Published by order of the Lords Commissioners of the Admiralty, 1858." They have since formed the subject of an elaborate Memoir by Messrs. Parker and Jones, published in the *Philosophical Transactions* for 1865.

dred miles from east to west, as well as we know that of any part of the dry land.

It is a prodigious plain — one of the widest and most even plains in the world. If the sea were drained off, you might drive a wagon all the way from Valentia, on the west coast of Ireland, to Trinity Bay, in Newfoundland. And, except upon one sharp incline about two hundred miles from Valentia, I am not quite sure that it would even be necessary to put the skid on, so gentle are the ascents and descents upon that long route. From Valentia the road would lie down-hill for about 200 miles to the point at which the bottom is now covered by 1700 fathoms of sea-water. Then would come the central plain, more than a thousand miles wide, the inequalities of the surface of which would be hardly perceptible, though the depth of water upon it now varies from 10,000 to 15,000 feet; and there are' places in which Mont Blanc might be sunk without showing its peak above water. Beyond this, the ascent on the American side commences, and gradually leads, for about 300 miles, to the Newfoundland shore.

Almost the whole of the bottom of this central plain (which extends for many hundred miles in a north and south direction) is covered by a fine mud, which, when brought to the surface, dries into a greyish-white friable substance. You can write with this on a blackboard, if you are so inclined; and, to the eye, it is quite like very soft, greyish chalk. Examined chemically, it proves to be composed almost wholly of carbonate of lime; and if you make a section of it, in the same way as that of the piece of chalk was made, and view it with the microscope, it presents innumerable *Globigerince* embedded in a granular matrix.

Thus this deep-sea mud is substantially chalk. I say substantially, because there are a good many minor differences; but as these have no bearing on the question immediately before us, — which is the nature of the *Globigerince* of the chalk, — it is unnecessary to speak of them.

Globigernice of every size, from the smallest to the largest, are associated together in the Atlantic mud, and the chambers of many are filled by a soft animal matter. This soft substance is, in fact, the remains of the creature to which the *Globigerina* shell, or rather akeleton, owes its existence — and which is an animal of the simplest imaginable description. It is, in fact, a mere particle of living jelly, without defined parts of any kind — without a mouth, nerves, muscles, or distinct organs, and only manifesting its vitality to ordinary observation by thrusting out and retracting from all parts of its surface, long filamentous processes, which serve for arms and legs. Yet this amorphous particle, devoid of everything which, in the higher animals, we call organs, is capable of feeding, growing and multiplying; of separating from the ocean the small proportion of carbonate of lime which is dissolved in sea-water; and of building up that substance into a skeleton for itself, according to a pattern which can be imitated by no other known agency.

The notion that animals can live and flourish in the sea, at the vast depths from which apparently living *Globigerince have been brought up, does not agree very well with our usual conceptions respecting the condi-tions of animal life; and it is not so absolutely impossible as it might at first appear to be, that the Globigerince* of the Atlantic sea-bottom do not live and die where they are found.

As I have mentioned, the soundings from the great Atlantic plain are almost entirely made up of *Globigerince,* with the granules which have been mentioned and some few other calcareous shells; but a small percentage of the chalky mud — perhaps at most some five per cent of it — is of a different nature, and consists of shells and skeletons composed of silex, or pure flint. These silicious bodies belong partly to the lowly vegetable organisms which are called *Diatomacece,* and partly to the minute, and extremely simple, animals, termed *Radiolaria.* It is quite certain that these creatures do not live at the bottom of the ocean, but at its surface — where they may be obtained in prodigious numbers by the use of a properly constructed net. Hence it follows that these silicious organisms, though they are not heavier than the lightest dust, must have fallen, in some cases, through fifteen thousand feet of water, before they reached their final resting-place on the ocean floor. And, considering how large a surface these bodies expose in proportion to their weight, it is probable that they occupy a great length , of time in making their burial journey from the surface of the Atlantic to the bottom.

But if the *Radiolaria* and Diatoms are thus rained upon the bottom of the sea, from the superficial layer of its waters in which they pass their lives, it is obviously possible that the *Globigerinoe* may be similarly derived; and if they were so, it would be much more easy to understand how they obtain their supply of food than it is at present. Nevertheless, the positive and negative evidence all points the other way. The skeletons of the full-grown, deep-sea Globigerinoe are so remarkably solid and heavy in proportion to their surface as to seem little fitted for floating; and, as a matter of fact, they are not to be found along with the Diatoms and Radiolaria, in the uppermost stratum of the open ocean.

It has been observed, again, that the abundance of *Globigerinæ, in proportion to other organisms, of like kind, increases with the depth of the sea; and that deep-water Globigerinæ* are larger than those which live in shallower parts of the sea; and such facts negative the supposition that these organisms have beat swept by currents from the shallows into the deeps of the Atlantic.

It therefore seems to be hardly doubtful that these wonderful creatures live and die at the depths in which they are found.

However, the important points for us are, that the living *Globigerinæ* are exclusively marine animals, the skeletons of which abound at the bottom of deep seas; and that there is not a shadow of reason for believing that the habits of the *Globigerinæ* of the chalk differed from those of the existing species. But if this be true, there is no escaping the conclusion that the chalk itself is the dried mud of an ancient deep sea.

In working over the soundings collected by Captain Dayman, I was surprised to find that many of what I have called the "granules" of that mud, were not, as one might have been tempted to think at first, the mere powder and waste of *Globigerinæ*, but that they had a definite form and size. I termed these bodies *"coccoliths"* and doubted their organic nature. Dr. Wallich verified my observation, and added the interesting discovery, that, not unfrequently, bodies similar to these " coccoliths " were aggregated together into spheroids, which he termed *"coccospheres."* So far as we knew, these bodies, the nature of which is extremely puzzling and problematical, were peculiar to the Atlantic soundings.

But, a few years ago, Mr. Sorby, in making a careful examination of the chalk by means of thin sections and otherwise, observed, as Ehrenberg had done before him, that much of its granular basis possesses a definite form. Comparing these formed particles with those in the Atlantic soundings, he found the two to be identical; and thus proved that the chalk, like the soundings, contains these mysterious coccoliths and coccospheres. Here was a further and a most interesting confirmation, from internal evidence, of the essential identity of the chalk with modern deep-sea mud. *Globigerinæ*, coccoliths, and coccospheres are found as the chief constituents of both, and testify to the general similarity of the conditions under which both have been formed.

The evidence furnished by the hewing, facing, and superposition of the stones of the Pyramids, that these structures were built by men, has no greater weight than the evidence that the chalk was built by *Globigerinœ*; and the belief that those ancient pyramid-builders were terrestrial and air-breathing creatures like ourselves, is it not better based than the conviction that the chalk-makers lived in the sea?

But as our belief in the building of the Pyramids by men is not only grounded on the internal evidences afforded by these structures, but gathers strength from multitudinous collateral proofs, and is clinched by the total absence of any reason for a contrary belief; so the evidence drawn from the *Gldrigerinœ* that the chalk is an ancient sea-bottom, is fortified by innumerable independent lines of evidence; and our belief in the truth of the conclusion to which all positive testimony tends, receives the like negative justification from the fact that no other hypothesis has a shadow of foundation.

It may be worth while briefly to consider a few of these collateral proofs that the chalk was deposited at the bottom of the sea.

The great mass of the chalk is composed, as we have seen, of the skeletons of *Globigerinœ*, and other simple organisms, imbedded in granular matter. Here and there, however, this hardened mud of the ancient sea reveals the remains of higher animals which have lived and died, and left their hard parts in the mud, just as the oysters die and leave their shells behind them, in the mud of the present seas.

There are, at the present day, certain groups of animals which are never found in fresh waters, being unable to live anywhere but in the sea. Such are the corals; those corallines which are called *Polycoa* ; those creatures which fabricate the lamp-shells, and are called *Brachiopoda*; the pearly Nautilus, and all animals allied to it; and all the forms of sear-urchins and star-fishes.

Not only are all these creatures confined to salt water at the present day; but, so far as our records of the past go, the conditions of their existence have been the same: hence, their occurrence in any deposit is as strong evidence as can be obtained, that that deposit was formed in the sea. Now the remains of animals of all the kinds which have been enumerated, occur in the chalk, in greater or less abundance; while not one of those forms of shell-fish which are characteristic of fresh water has yet been observed in it.

When we consider that the remains of more than three thousand distinct species of aquatic animals have been discovered among the fossils of the chalk, that the great majority of them are of such forms as are now met with only in the sea, and that there is no reason to believe that any one of them inhabited fresh water — the collateral evidence that the chalk represents an ancient sea-bottom acquires as great force as the proof derived from the nature of the chalk itself. I think you will now allow that I did not overstate my case when I asserted that we' have as strong grounds for believing that all the vast area of dry land, at present occupied by the chalk, was once at the bottom of the sea, as we have for any matter of history whatever; while there is no justification for any other belief.

No less certain it is that the time, during which the countries we now call south-east England, France, Germany, Poland, Russia, Egypt, Arabia, Syria, were more or less completely covered by a deep sea, was of considerable duration.

We have already seen that the chalk is, in places, more than a thousand feet thick. I think you will agree with me, that it must have taken some time for the skeletons of animalcules of a hundredth of an inch in diameter to heap up such a mass as that. I have said that throughout the thickness of the chalk the remains of other animals are scattered. These remains are often in the most exquisite state of preservation. The valves of the shell-fishes are commonly adherent; the long spines of some of the sea-urchins, which would be detached by the smallest jar, often remain in their places. In a word, it is certain that these animals have lived and died when the place which they now occupy was the surface of as much of the chalk as had then been deposited; and that each has been covered up by the layer of *Globigerina* mud, upon which the creatures imbedded a little higher up have, in like manner, lived and died. But some of these remains prove the existence of reptiles of vast size in the chalk sea. These lived their time, and had their ancestors and descendants, which assuredly implies time, reptiles being of slow growth.

There is more curious evidence, again, that the process of covering up, or, in other words, the deposit of *Globigerina* skeletons, did not go on very fast. It is demonstrable that an animal of the cretaceous sea might die, that its skeleton might lie uncovered upon the sea-bottom long enough to lose all its outward coverings and appendages by putrefaction; and that, after this had happened, another animal might attach itself to the dead and naked skeleton, might grow to maturity, and might itself die before the calcareous mud had buried the whole.

Cases of this kind are admirably described by Sir Charles Lyell. He speaks of the frequency with which geologists find in the chalk a fossilized sea-urchin, to which is attached the lower valve of a *Crania*. This is a kind of shell-fish, with a shell composed of two pieces, of which, as in the oyster, one is fixed and the other free.

"The upper valve is almost invariably wanting, though occasionally found in a perfect state of preservation in the white chalk at some distance. In this case, we see clearly that the sea-urchin first lived from youth to age, then died and lost its spines, which were carried away. Then the young *Crania* adhered to the bared shell, grew and perished in its turn; after which, the upper valve was separated from the lower, before the Echinus became enveloped in chalky mud."

A specimen in the Museum of Practical Geology, in London, still further prolongs the period which must have elapsed between the death of the sea-urchin, and its burial by the *Globigerince*. For the outward face of the valve of a *Crania*, which is attached to a sea-urchin (*Micraster*), is itself overrun by an incrusting coralline, which spreads thence over more or less of the surface of the sea-urchin. It follows that, after the upper valve of the *Crania* fell off, the surface of the attached valve must have remained exposed long enough to allow of the growth of the whole coralline, since corallines do not live imbedded in mud.

The progress of knowledge may, one day, enable us to deduce from such facts as these the maximum rate at which the chalk can have accumulated, and thus to arrive at the minimum duration of the chalk period. Suppose that the valve of the *Crania* upon which a coralline has fixed itself in the way just described, is so attached to the sea-urchin that no part of it is more than an inch above the face upon which the sea-urchin rests. Then, as the coralline could not have fixed itself, if the *Crania* had been covered up with chalk mud, and could not have lived had itself been so covered it follows, that an inch of chalk mud could not have accumulated within the time between the death and decay of the soft parts of the sea-urchin and the growth of the coralline to the full size which it has attained. If the decay of the soft parts of the sea-urchin; the attachment, growth to maturity, and decay of the *Crania*; and the subsequent attachment and growth of the coralline, took a year (which is a low estimate enough), the accumulation of the inch of chalk must have taken more than a year: and the deposit of a thousand feet of chalk must, consequently, have taken more than twelve thousand years.

The foundation of all this calculation is, of course, a knowledge of the length of time the *Crania* and the coralline needed to attain their full size; and, on this head, precise knowledge is at present wanting. But there are circumstances which tend to show, that nothing like an inch of chalk has accumulated during the life of a *Crania* ; and, on any probable estimate of the length of that life, the chalk period must have had a much longer duration than that thus roughly as-signed to it.

Thus, not only is it certain that the chalk is the mud of an ancient sea-bottom; but it is no less certain, that the chalk sea existed during an extremely long period, though we may not be prepared to give a precise estimate of the length of that period in years. The relative duration is clear, though the absolute duration may not be definable. The attempt to affix any precise date to the period at which the chalk sea began, or ended, its existence, is baffled by difficulties of the same kind. But the relative age of the cretaceous epoch may be determined with as great ease and certainty as the long duration of that epoch.

You will have heard of the interesting discoveries recently made, in various parts of Western Europe, of flint implements, obviously worked into shape by human hands, under circumstances which show conclusively that man is a very ancient denizen of these re-gions.

It has been proved that the old populations of Europe, whose existence has been revealed to us in this way, consisted of savages, such as the Esquimaux are now; that, in the country which is now France, they hunted the reindeer, and were familiar with the ways of the mammoth and the bison. The physical geography of France was in those days different from what it is now — the river Somme, for instance, having cut its bed a hundred feet deeper between that time and this; and, it is probable, that the climate was more like that of Canada or Siberia, than that of Western Europe.

The existence of these people is forgotten even in the traditions of the oldest historical nations. The name and fame of them had utterly vanished until a few years back; and the amount of physical change which has been effected since their day, renders it more than probable that, venerable as are some of the historical nations, the workers of the chipped flints of Hoxne or of Amiens are to them, as they are to us, in point of antiquity.

But, if we assign to these hoar relics of long-vanished generations of men the greatest age that can possibly be claimed for them, they are not older than the drift, or boulder clay, which, in comparison with the chalk, is but a very juvenile deposit. You need go no further than your own sea-board for evidence of this fact. At one of the most charming spots on the coast of Norfolk, Cromer, you will see the boulder clay forming a vast mass, which lies upon the chalk, and must consequently have come into existence after it. Huge boulders of chalk are, in fact, included in the clay, and have evidently been brought to the position they now occupy, by the same agency as that which has planted blocks of syenite from Norway side by side with them.

The chalk, then, is certainly older than the boulder clay. If you ask how much, I will again take you no further than the same spot upon your own coasts for evidence. I have spoken of the boulder clay and drift as resting upon the chalk. That is not strictly true. Interposed between the chalk and the drift is a comparatively insignificant layer, containing vegetable matter. But that layer tells a wonderful history. It is full of stumps of trees standing as they grew. Fir-trees are there with their cones, and hazel-bushes with their nuts; there stand the stools of oak and yew trees, beeches and alders. Hence this stratum is appropriately called the "forest-bed."

It is obvious that the chalk must have been upheaved and converted into dry land, before the timber trees could grow upon it. As the boles of some of these trees are from two to three feet in diameter, it is no less clear that the dry land this formed remained in the same condition for long ages. And not only do the remains of stately oaks and well-grown firs testify to the duration of this condition of things, but additional evidence to the same effect is afforded by the abundant remains of elephants, rhinoceroses, hippopotomuses and other great wild beasts, which it has yielded to the aealous search of such men as the Rev. Mr. Gunn.

When you look at such a collection as he has formed, and bethink you that these elephantine bones did veri-tably carry their owners about, and these great grinders crunch, in the dark woods of which the forest-bed is now the only trace, it is impossible not to feel that they are as good evidence of the lapse of time as the annual rings of the tree-stumps.

Thus there is a writing upon the walls of cliffs at Cromer. and whoso runs may read it. It tells us, with All authority which cannot be impeached, that the aucient sea-bed of the chalk sea was raised up, and muained dry land, until it was covered with forest, stocked with the great game whose spoils have rejoiced your geologists. How long it remained in that condition cannot be said; but " the whirligig of time brought its revenges" in those days as in these. That dry land, with the bones and teeth of generations of long-lived elephants hidden away among the gnarled roots and dry leaves of its ancient trees, sank gradually to the bottom of the icy sea, which covered it with huge masses of drift and boulder clay. Sea-beasts, such as the wal-rus, now restricted to the extreme north, paddled about where birds had twittered among the topmost twigs of the fir-trees. How long this state of things endured we know not, but at length it came to an end. The upheaved glacial mud hardened into the soil of modern Norfolk. Forests grew once more, the wolf and the beaver replaced the reindeer and the elephant; and at length what we call the history of England dawned.

Thus you have within the limits of your own county, proof that the chalk can justly claim a very much greater antiquity than even the oldest physical traces of mankind. But we may go further and demonstrate, by evidence of the same author-ity as that which testifies to the existence of the father of men, that the chalk is vastly older than Adam himself.

The Book of Genesis informs us that Adam, imme-diately upon his creation, and before the appearance of Eve, was placed in the Garden of Eden. The problem of the geographical position of Eden has greatly vexed the spirits of the learned in such matters, but there is one point respecting which, so far as I know, no com-mentator has ever raised a doubt. This is, that of the four rivers which are said to run out of it, Euphrates and Hiddekel are identical with the rivers now known by the names of Euphrates and Tigris.

But the whole country in which these mighty rivers take their origin, and through which they run, is composed of rocks which are either of the same age as the chalk, or of later date. So that the chalk must not only have been formed, but, after its formation, the time required for the deposit of these later rocks, and for their upheaval into dry land, must have elapsed, before the smallest brook which feeds the swift stream of "the great river, the river of Babylon," began to flow.

Thus, evidence which cannot be rebutted, and which need not be strengthened, though if time permitted I might indefinitely increase its quantity, compels you to believe that the earth, from the time of the chalk to the present day, has been the theatre of a series of changes as vast in their amount, as they were slow in their progress. The area on which we stand has been first sea and then land, for at least four alternations; and has remained in each of these conditions for a period of great length.

Nor have these wonderful metamorphoses of sea into land, and of land into sea, been confined to one corner of England. During the chalk period, or "cretaceous epoch," not one of the present great physical features of the globe was in existence. Our great mountain ranges, Pyrenees, Alps, Himalayas, Andes, have all been up-heaved since the chalk was deposited, and the cretaceous sea flowed over the sites of Sinai and Ararat.

All this is certain, because rocks of cretaceous, or still later date have shared in the elevatory movements which gave rise to these mountain chains; and may be found perched up, in some cases, many thousand feet high upon their flanks. And evidence of equal cogency demonstrates that, though, in Norfolk, the forest-bed rests directly upon the chalk, yet it does so, not because the period at which the forest grew immediately followed that at which the chalk was formed, but because an immense lapse of time, represented elsewhere by thousands of feet of rock, is not indicated at Cromer.

I must ask you to believe that there is no less conclusive proof that a still more prolonged succession of similar changes occurred, before the chalk was deposited. Nor have we any reason to think that the first term in the series of these changes is known. The oldest sea-beds preserved to us are sands, and mud, and pebbles, the wear and tear of rocks which were formed in still older oceans.

But, great as is the magnitude of these physical changes of the world, they have been accompanied by a no less striking series of modifications in its living inhabitants.

All the great classes of animals, beasts of the field, fowls of the air, creeping things, and things which dwell in the waters, flourished upon the globe long ages before the chalk was deposited. Very few, however, if any, of these ancient forms of animal life were identical with those which now live. Certainly not one of the higher animals was of the same species as any of those now in existence. The beasts of the field, in the days before the chalk, were not our beasts of the field, nor the fowls of the air such as those which the eye of men has seen flying, unless his antiquity dates infinitely further back than we at present surmise. If we could be carried back into those times, we should be as one suddenly set down in Australia before it was colonized. We should see mammals, birds, reptiles, fishes, insects, snails, and the like, clearly recognisable as such, and yet not one of them would be just the same as those with which we are familiar, and many would be extremely different.

From that time to the present, the population of the world has undergone slow and gradual, but incessant changes. There has been no grand catastrophe — no destroyer has swept away the forms of life of one period, and replaced them by a totally new creation; but one species has vanished and another has taken its place; creatures of one type of structure have diminished, those of another have increased, as time has passed on. And thus, while the differences between the living creatures of the time before the chalk and those of the present day appear startling, if placed side by side, we are led from one to the other by the most gradual progress, if we follow the course of Nature through the whole series of those relics of her operations which she has left behind.

And it is by the population of the chalk sea that the ancient and the modern inhabitants of the world are most completely connected. The groups which are dying out flourish, side by side, with the groups which are now the dominant forms of life.

Thus the chalk contains remains of those strange flying and swimming reptiles, the pterodactyl, the ichthyosaurus, and the plesiosaurus, which are found in no later deposits, but abounded in preceding ages. The chambered shells called ammonites and belemnites, which are so characteristic of the period preceding the cretaceous, in like manner die with it.

But, amongst these fading remainders of a previous state of things, are some very modern forms of life, looking like Yankee pedlars among a tribe of Red Indians. Crocodiles of modern type appear; bony fishes, many of them very similar to existing species almost supplant the forms of fish which predominate in more ancient seas; and many kinds of living shellfish first become known to us in the chalk. The vegetation acquires a modern aspect. A few living animals are not even distinguishable as species, from those which existed at that remote epoch. The *Globigerina* of the present day, for example, is not different specifically from that of the chalk; and the same may be said of many other *Foraminifera*. I think it probable that critical and unprejudiced examination will show that more than one species of much higher animals have had a similar longevity; but the only example, which I can at present give confidently is the snake's-head lamp-shell (*Terebratulina caput serpentis*), which lives in our English seas and abounded (as *Tere-bratulina striata* of authors) in the chalk.

The longest line of human ancestry must hide its diminished head before the pedigree of this insignifi-cant shell-fish. We Englishmen are proud to have an ancestor who was present at the Battle of Hastings. The ancestors of *Terebratvlina caput serpentis* may have been present at a battle of *Ichthyosauria* in that part of the sea which, when the chalk was forming, flowed over the site of Hastings. While all around has changed, this *Terebratulina* has peacefully propagated its species from generation to generation, and stands to this day, as a living testimony to the continuity of the present with the past history of the globe.

Up to this moment I have stated, so far as I know, nothing but well-authenticated facts, and the immediate conclusions which they force upon the mind.

But the mind is so constituted that it does not willingly rest in facts and immediate causes, but seeks always alter a knowledge of the remoter links in the chain of causation.

Taking the many changes of any given spot of the earth's surface, from sea to land and from land to sea, as an established fact, we cannot refrain from asking ourselves how these changes have occurred. And when we have explained them — as they most be explained — by the alternate slow movements of elevation and depression which have affected the crust of the earth, we go still further back, and ask, Why these movements?

I am not certain that any one can give you a satis-factory answer to that question. Assuredly I cannot. All that can be said, for certain, is, that such movements are part of the ordinary course of nature, inasmuch as they are going on at the present time. Direct proof may be given, that some parts of the land of the northern hemisphere are at this moment insensibly rising and others insensibly sinking; and there is indirect, but perfectly satisfactory, proof, that an enormous area now covered by the Pacific has been deepened thousands of feet, since the present inhabitants of that sea came into existence.

Thus there is not a shadow of a reason for believing that the physical changes of the globe, in past times have been effected by other than natural causes.

Is there any more reason for believing that the concomitant modifications in the forms of the living inhabitants of the globe have been brought about in other ways ?

Before attempting to answer this question, let us try to form a distinct mental picture of what has happened, in some special case.

The crocodiles are animals which, as a group, have a very vast antiquity. They abounded ages before the chalk was deposited; they throng the rivers in warm climates, at the present day. There is a difference in the form of the joints of the backbone, and in some minor particulars, between the crocodiles of the present epoch and those which lived before the chalk; but, in the cretaceous epoch, as I have already mentioned, the crocodiles had assumed the modern type of structure. Notwithstanding this, the crocodiles of the chalk are not identically the same as those which lived in the times called "older tertiary," which succeeded the cretaceous epoch; and the crocodiles of the older tertiaries are not identical with those of the newer tertiaries, nor are these identical with existing forms. I leave open the question whether particular species may have lived on from epoch to epoch. But each epoch has had its peculiar crocodiles; though all, since the chalk, have belonged to the modern type, and differ simply in their proportions, and in such structural particulars as are discernible only to trained eyes.

How is the existence of this long succession of different species of crocodiles to be accounted for ?

Only two suppositions seem to be open to us — Either each species of crocodile has been specially created, or it has arisen out of some pre-existing form by the operation of natural causes.

Choose your hypothesis; I have chosen mine. I can find no warranty for believing in the distinct creation of a score of successive species of crocodiles in the course of countless ages of time. Science gives no countenance to such a wild fancy; nor can even the perverse ingenuity of a commentator pretend to discover this sense, in the simple words in which the writer of Genesis records the proceedings of the fifth and sixth days of the Creation.

On the other hand, I see no good reason for doubting the necessary alternative, that all these varied species have been evolved from pre-existing crocodilian forms, by the operation of causes as completely a part of the common order of nature, as those which have effected the changes of the inorganic world.

Few will venture to affirm that the reasoning which applies to crocodiles loses its force among other animals, or among plants. If one series of species has come into existence by the operation of natural causes, it seems folly to deny that all may have arisen in the same way.

A small beginning has led us to a great ending. If I were to put the bit of chalk with which we started into the hot but obscure flame of burning hydrogen, it would presently shine like the sun. It seems to me that this physical metamorphosis is no false image of what has been the result of our subjecting it to a jet of fer-vent, though nowise brilliant, thought to-night. It has become luminous, and its clear rays, penetrating the abyss of the remote past, have brought within our ken some stages of the evolution of the earth. And in the shifting "without haste, but without rest" of the land and sea, as in the endless variation of the forms assumed by living beings, we have observed nothing but the natural product of the forces originally possessed by the substance of the universe.

THE PRINCIPAL SUBJECT OF EDUCATION

I KNOW quite well that launching myself into this discussion is a very danger-ous operation; that it is a very large subject, and one which is difficult to deal with, however much I may trespass upon your patience in the time allotted to me. But the discussion is so fundamental, it is so completely impossible to make up one's mind on these matters until one has settled the question, that I will even venture to make the experiment. A great lawyer-statesman and philosopher of a former age — I mean Francis Bacon — said that truth came out of error much more rapidly than it came out of confusion. There is a wonderful truth in that saying. Next to being right in this world, the best of all things is to be clearly and definitely wrong, because you will come out somewhere. If you go buzzing about between right and wrong, vibrating and fluctuating, you come out nowhere; but if you are absolutely and thoroughly and persistently wrong, you must, some of these days, have the extreme good fortune of knocking your head against a fact, and that sets you all straight again. So I will not trouble myself as to whether I may be right or wrong in what I am about to say, but at any rate I hope to be clear and definite; and then you will be able to judge for yourselves whether, in following out the train of thought I have to introduce, you knock your heads against facts or not.

I take it that the whole object of education is, in the first place, to train the faculties of the young in such a manner as to give their possessors the best chance of being happy and useful in their generation; and, in the second place, to furnish them with the most important portions of that immense capitalised experience of the human race which we call knowledge of various kinds. I am using the term knowledge in its widest possible sense; and the question is, what subjects to select by training and discipline, in which the object I have just defined may be best attained.

I must call your attention further to this fact, that all the subjects of our thoughts — all feelings and propo-sitions (leaving aside our sensations as the mere materials and occasions of thinking and feeling), all our mental furniture — may be classified under one of two heads — as either within the province of the intellect, something that can be put into propositions and affirmed or denied; or as within the province of feeling, or that which, before the name was defiled, was called the Aesthetic side of our nature, and which can neither be proved nor disproved, but only felt and known.

According to the classification which I have put before you, then, the subjects of all knowledge are divisible into the two groups, matters of science and matters of art; for all things with which the reasoning faculty alone is occupied, come under the province of science; and in the broadest sense, and not in the narrow and technical sense in which we are now accustomed to use the word art, all things feelable, all things which stir our emotions, come under the term of art, in the sense of the subject-matter of the aesthetic faculty. So that we are shut up to this — that the business of education is, in the first place, to provide the young with the means and the habit of observation; and, secondly, to supply the subject-matter of knowledge either in the shape of science or of art, or of both combined.

Now, it is a very remarkable fact — but it is true of most things in this world — that there is hardly anything one-sided, or of one nature; and it is not immediately obvious what of the things that interest us may be regarded as pure science, and what may be regarded as pure art. It may be that there are some peculiarly constituted persons who, before they have advanced far into the depths of geometry, find artistic beauty about it; but, taking the generality of mankind, I think it may be said that, when they begin to learn mathematics, their whole souls are absorbed in tracing the connection between the premises and the conclusion, and that to them geometry is pure science. So I think it may be said that mechanics and osteology are pure science. On the other hand, melody in music is pure art. You cannot reason about it; there is no proposition involved in it. So, again, in the pictorial art, an arabesque, or a "harmony in grey," touches none but the aesthetic faculty. But a great mathematician, and even many persons who are not great mathematicians, will tell you that they derive immense pleasure from geometrical reasonings. Everybody knows mathematicians speak of solutions and problems as " elegant," and they tell you that a certain mass of mystic symbols is "beautiful, quite lovely." Well, you do not see it. They do see it, because the intellectual process, the process of comprehending the reasons symbolised by these figures and these signs, confers upon them a sort of pleasure, such as an artist has in visual symmetry. Take a science of which I may speak with more confidence, and which is the most attractive of those I am concerned with. It is what we call morphology, which consists in tracing out the unity in variety of the infinitely diversified structures of animals and plants. I cannot give you any example of a thorough aesthetic pleasure more intensely real than a pleasure of this kind — the pleasure which arises in one's mind when a whole mass of different structures run into one harmony as the expression of a central law. That is where the province of art overlays and embraces the province of intellect. And, if I may venture to express an opinion on such a subject, the great majority of forms of art are not in the sense what I just now defined them to be — pure art; but they derive much of their quality from simultaneous and even unconscious excitement of the intellect.

When I was a boy, I was very fond of music, and I am so now; and it so happened that I had the opportunity of hearing much good music. Among other things, I had abundant opportunities of hearing that great old master, Sebastian Bach. I remember perfectly well — though I knew nothing about music then, and, I may add, know nothing whatever about it now — the intense satisfaction and delight which I had in listening, by the hour together, to Bach's fugues. It is a pleasure which remains with me, I am glad to think; but, of late years, I have tried to find out the why and wherefore, and it has often occurred to me that the pleasure derived from musical compositions of this kind is essentially of the same nature as that which is derived from pursuits which are commonly regarded as purely intellectual. I mean, that the source of pleasure is exactly the same as in most of my problems in mor-pho-logy—that you have the theme in one of the old master's works followed out in all its endless variations, always appearing and always reminding you of unity in variety. So in painting; what is called "truth to nature" is the intellectual element coming in, and truth to nature depends entirely upon the intellectual culture of the person to whom art is addressed. If you are in Australia, you may get credit for being a good artist — I mean among the natives — if you can draw a kangaroo after a fashion. But, among men of higher civilisation, the intellectual knowledge we possess brings its criticism into our appreciation of works of art, and we are obliged to satisfy it, as well as the mere sense of beauty in colour and in outline. And so, the higher the culture and information of those whom art addresses, the more exact and precise must be what we call its "truth to nature."

If we turn to literature, the same thing is true, and you find works of literature which may be said to be pure art. A little song of Shakespeare or of Goethe is pure art; it is exquisitely beautiful, although its intellectual content may be nothing. A series of pictures is made to pass before your mind by the meaning of words, and the effect is a melody of ideas. Nevertheless, the great mass of the literature we esteem is valued, not merely because of having artistic form, but because of its intellectual content; and the value is the higher the more precise, distinct, and true is that intellectual content. And, if you will let me for a moment speak of the very highest forms of literature, do we not regard them as highest simply because the more we know the truer they seem, and the more competent we are to appreciate beauty the more beautiful they are ? No man ever understands Shakespeare until he is old, though the youngest may admire him, the reason being that he satisfies the artistic instinct of the youngest and harmonises with the ripest and richest experience of the oldest.

I have said this much to draw your attention to what, in my mind, lies at the root of all this matter, and at the understanding of one another by the men of science on the one hand, and the men of literature, and history, and art, on the other. It is not a question whether one order of study or another should predominate. It is a question of what topics of education you shall select which will combine all the needful elements in such due proportion as to give the greatest amount of food, support, and encouragement to those faculties which enable us to appreciate truth, and to profit by those sources of innocent happiness which are open to us, and, at the same time, to avoid that which is bad, and coarse, and ugly, and keep clear of the multitude of pitfalls and dangers which beset those who break through the natural or moral laws.

I address myself, in this spirit, to the consideration of the question of the value of purely literary education. Is it good and sufficient, or is it insufficient and bad ? Well, here I venture to say that there are literary educations and literary educations. If I am to understand by that term the education that was current in the great majority of middle-class schools, and upper schools too, in this country when I was a boy, and which consisted absolutely and almost entirely in keeping boys for eight or ten years at learning the rules of Latin and Greek grammar, construing certain Latin and Greek authors, and possibly making verses which, had they been English verses, would have been condemned as abominable doggerel, — if that is what you mean by liberal education, then I say it is scandalously insufficient and almost worthless. My reason for saying so is not from the point of view of science at all, but from the point of view of literature. I say the thing professes to be literary education that is not a literary education at all. It was not literature at all that was taught, but science in a very bad form. It is quite obvious that grammar is science and not literature. The analysis of a text by the help of the rules of grammar is just as much a scientific operation as the analysis of a chemical compound by the help of the rules of chemical analysis. There is nothing that appeals to the aesthetic faculty in that operation; and I ask multitudes of men of my own age, who went through this process, whether they ever had a conception, of art or literature until they obtained it for themselves after leaving school? Then you may say, " If that is so, if the education was scientific, why cannot you be satisfied with it ? " I say, because although it is a scientific training, it is of the most inadequate and inappropriate kind. If there is any good at all in scientific education it is that men should be trained, as I said before, to know things for themselves at first hand, and that they should understand every step of the reason of that which they do.

I desire to speak with the utmost respect of that science — philology — of which grammar is a part and parcel; yet everybody knows that grammar, as it is usually learned at school, affords no scientific training. It is taught just as you would teach the rules of chess or draughts. On the other hand, if I am to understand by a literary education the study of the literatures of either ancient or modern nations — but especially those of antiquity, and especially that of ancient Greece; if this literature is studied, not merely from the point of view of philological science, and its practical application to the interpretation of texts, but as an exemplification of and commentary upon the principles of art; if you look upon the literature of a people as a chapter in the development of the human mind, if you work out this in a broad spirit, and with such collateral references to morals and politics, and physical geography, and the like as are needful to make you comprehend what the meaning of ancient literature and civilisation is, — then, assuredly, it affords a splendid and noble education. But I still think it is susceptible of improvement, and that no man will ever comprehend the real secret of the difference between the ancient world and our present time, unless he has learned to see the difference which the late development of physical science has made between the thought of this day and the thought of that, and he will never see that difference, unless he has some practical insight into some branches of physical science; and you must remember that a literary education such as that which I have just referred to, is out of the reach of those whose school life is cut short at sixteen or seventeen.

But, you will say, all this is fault-finding; let us hear what you have in the way of positive suggestion. Then I am bound to tell you that, if I could make a clean sweep of everything — I am very glad I cannot because I might, and probably should, make mistakes, — but if I could make a clean sweep of everything and start afresh, I should, in the first place, secure that training of the young in reading and writing, and in the habit of attention and observation, both to that which is told them, and that which they see, which everybody agrees to. But in addition to that, I should make it absolutely necessary for everybody, for a longer or shorter period, to learn to draw. Now, you may say, there are some people who cannot draw, however much they may be taught. I deny that *in toto,* because I never yet met with anybody who could not learn to write. Writing is a form of drawing; therefore if you give the same attention and trouble to drawing as you do to writing, depend upon it, there is nobody who cannot be made to draw, more or less well. Do not misapprehend me. I do not say for one moment you would make an artistic draughtsman. Artists are not made; they grow. You may improve the natural faculty in that direction, but you cannot make it; but you can teach simple drawing, and you will find it an implement of learning of extreme value. I do not think its value can be exaggerated, because it gives you the means of training the young in attention and accuracy, which are the two things in which all mankind are more deficient than in any other mental quality whatever. The whole of my life has been spent in trying to give my proper at-tention to things and to be accurate, and I have not succeeded as well as I could wish; and other people, I am afraid, are not much more fortunate. You cannot begin this habit too early, and I consider there is nothing of so great a value as the habit of drawing, to secure those two desirable ends.

Then we come to the subject-matter, whether scientific or aesthetic, of education, and I should naturally have no question at all about teaching the elements of physical science of the kind I have sketched, in a practical manner; but among scientific topics, using the word scientific in the broadest sense, I would also include the elements of the theory of morals and of that of political and social life, which, strangely enough, it never seems to occur to anybody to teach a child. I would have the history of our own country, and of all the influences which have been brought to bear upon it, with incidental geography, not as a mere chronicle of reigns and battles, but as a chapter in the development of the race, and the history of civilisation.

Then with respect to aesthetic knowledge and discipline, we have happily in the English language one of the most magnificent storehouses of artistic beauty and of models of literary excellence which exists in the world at the present time. I have said before, and I repeat it here, that if a man cannot get literary culture of the .highest kind out of his Bible, and Chaucer, and Shakespeare, and Milton, and Hobbes, and Bishop Berkeley, to mention only a few of our illustrious writers — I say, if he cannot get it out of those writers he cannot get it out of anything; and I would assuredly devote a very large portion of the time of every English child to the careful study of the models of English writing of such varied and wonderful kind as we possess, and, what is still more important and still more neglected, the habit of using that language with precision, with force, and with art. I fancy we are almost the only nation in the world who seem to think that composition comes by nature. The French attend to their own language, the Germans study theirs; but Englishmen do not seem to think it is worth their while. Nor would I fail to include, in the course of study I am sketching, translations of all the best works of antiquity, or of the modern world. It is a very desirable thing to read Homer in Greek; but if you don't happen to know Greek, the next best thing we can do is to read as good a translation of it as we have recently been furnished with in prose. You won't get all you would get from the original, but you may get a great deal; and to refuse to know this great deal because you cannot get all, seems -to be as sensible as for a hungry man to refuse bread because he cannot get partridge. Finally, I would add instruction in either music or painting, or, if the child should be so unhappy, as sometimes happens, as to have no faculty for either of those, and no possibility of doing anything in any artistic sense with them, then I would see what could be done with literature alone; but I would provide, in the fullest sense, for the development of the aesthetic side of the mind. In my judgment, those are all the essentials of education for an English child. With that outfit, such as it might be made in the time given to education which is within the reach of nine-tenths of the population — with that outfit, an Englishman, within the limits of English life, is fitted to go anywhere, to occupy the highest positions, to fill the highest offices of the State, and to become distinguished in practical pursuits, in science, or in art. For, if he have the opportunity to learn all those things, and have his mind disciplined in the various directions the teaching of those topics would have necessitated, then, assuredly, he will be able to pick up, on his road through life, all the rest of the intellectual baggage he wants.

If the educational time at our disposition were suffi-cient, there are one or two things I would add to those I have just now called the essentials; and perhaps you will be surprised to hear, though I hope you will not, that I should add, not more science, but one, or, if possible, two languages. The knowledge of some other language than one's own is, in fact, of singular intellectual value. Many of the faults and mistakes of the ancient philosophers are traceable to the fact that they knew no language but their own, and were often led into confusing the symbol with the thought which it embodied. I think it is Locke who says that one-half of the mistakes of philosophers have arisen from questions about words; and one of the safest ways of delivering yourself from the bondage of words is, to know how ideas look in words to which you are not accustomed. That is one reason for the study of language; another reason is, that it opens new fields in art and in science. Another is the practical value of such knowledge; and yet another is this, that if your languages are properly chosen, from the time of learning the additional languages you will know your own language better than ever you did. So, I say, if the time given to education permits, add Latin and German. Latin, because it is the key to nearly one-half of English and to all the Romance languages; and German, because it is the key to almost all the remainder of English, and helps you to understand a race from whom most of us have sprung, and who have a character and a literature of a fateful force in the history of the world, such as probably has been allotted to those of no other people, except the Jews, the Greeks, and ourselves. Beyond these, the essential and the eminently desirable elements of all education, let each man take up his special line — the historian devote himself to his history, the man of science to his science, the man of letters to his culture of that kind, and the artist to his special pursuit.

Bacon has prefaced some of his works with no more than this: *Franciscus Bacon sic cogitavit;* let " sic cogitavi" be the epilogue to what I have ventured to ad-dress to you to-night.

THE METHOD OF SCIENTIFIC INVESTIGATION

THE method of scientific investigation is nothing but the expression of the necessary mode of working of the human mind. It is simply the mode at which all phenomena are reasoned about, rendered precise and exact. There is no more difference, but there is just the same kind of difference, between the mental operations of a man of science and those of an ordinary person, as there is between the operations and methods of a baker or of a butcher weighing out his goods in common scales, and the operations of a chemist in performing a difficult and complex analysis by means of his balance and finely graduated weights. It is not that the action of the scales in the one case, and the balance in the other, differ in the principles of their construction or manner of working; but the beam of one is set on an infinitely finer axis than the other, and of course turns by the addition of a much smaller weight.

You will understand this better, perhaps, if I give you some familiar example. You have all heard it repeated, I dare say, that men of science work by means of induction and deduction, and that by the help of these operations, they, in a sort of sense, wring from Nature certain other things, which are called natural laws, and causes, and that out of these, by some cunning skill of their own, they build up hypotheses and theories. And it is imagined by many, that the operations of the common mind can be by no means compared with these processes, and that they have to be acquired by a sort of special apprenticeship to the craft. To hear all these large words, you would think that the mind of a man of science must be constituted differently from that of his fellow men; but if you will not be frightened by terms, you will discover that you are quite wrong, and that all these terrible apparatus are being used by yourselves every day and every hour of your lives.

There is a well-known incident in one of Molière's plays, where the author makes the hero express unbounded delight on being told that he had been talking prose during the whole of his life. In the same way, I trust, that you will take comfort, and be delighted with yourselves, on the discovery that you have been acting on the principles of inductive and deductive philosophy during the same period. Probably there is not one here who has not in the course of the day had occasion to set in motion a complex train of reasoning, of the very same kind, though differing of course in degree, as that which a scientific man goes through in tracing the causes of natural phenomena.

A very trivial circumstance will serve to exemplify this. Suppose you go into a fruiterer's shop, wanting an apple, — you take up one, and, on biting it, you find it is sour; you look at it, and see that it is hard and green. You take up another one, and that too is hard, green, and sour. The shopman offers you a third; but, before biting it, you examine it, and find that it is hard and green, and you immediately say that you will not have it, as it must be sour, like those that you have already tried.

Nothing can be more simple than that, you think; but if you will take the trouble to analyse and trace out into its logical elements what has been done by the mind, you will be greatly surprised. In the first place you have performed the operation of induction. You found that, in two experiences, hardness and greenness in apples went together with sourness. It was so in the first case, and it was confirmed by the second. True, it is a very small basis, but still it is enough to make an induction from; you generalise the facts, and you expect to find sourness in apples where you get hardness and greenness. You found upon that a general law that all hard and green apples are sour; and that, so far as it goes, is a perfect induction. Well, having got your natural law in this way, when you are offered another apple which you find is hard and green, you say, "All hard and green apples are sour; this apple is hard and green, therefore this apple is sour." That train of reasoning is what logicians call a syllogism, and has all its various parts and terms, — its major premiss, its minor premiss and its conclusion. And, by the help of further reasoning, which, if drawn out, would have to be exhibited in two or three other syllogisms, you arrive at your final determination, " I will not have that apple." So that, you see, you have, in the first place, established a law by induction, and upon that you have founded a deduction, and reasoned out the special particular case. Well now, suppose, having got your conclusion of the law, that at some time afterwards, you are discussing the qualities of apples with a friend: you will say to him, " It is a very curious thing, — but I find that all hard and green apples are sour!" Your friend says to you, " But how do you know that ? " You at once reply, " Oh, because I have tried them over and over again, and have always found them to be so." Well, if we were talking science instead of common sense, we should call that an experimental verification. And, if still opposed, you go further, and say, "I have heard from the people in Somersetshire and Devonshire, where a large number of apples are grown, that they have observed the same thing. It is also found to be the case in Normandy, and in North America. In short, I find it to be the universal experience of mankind wherever attention has been directed to the subject." Whereupon, your friend, unless he is a very unreasonable man, agrees with you, and is convinced that you are quite right in the conclusion you have drawn. He believes, although perhaps he does not know he believes it, that the more extensive verifications are, — that the more frequently experiments have been made, and results of the same kind arrived at, — that the more varied the conditions under which the same results are attained, the more certain is the ultimate conclusion, and he disputes the question no further. He sees that the experiment has been tried under all sorts of conditions, as to time, place, and people, with the same result; and he says with you, therefore, that the law you have laid down must be a good one, and he must believe it.

In science we do the same thing; — the philosopher exercises precisely the same faculties, though in a much more delicate manner. In scientific inquiry it becomes a matter of duty to expose a supposed law to every possible kind of verification, and to take care, moreover, that this is done intentionally, and not left to a mere accident, as in the case of the apples. And in science, as in common life, our confidence in a law is in exact proportion to the absence of variation in the result of our experimental verifications. For instance, if you let go your grasp of an article you may have in your hand, it will immediately fall to the ground. That is a very common verification of one of the best established laws of nature — that of gravitation. The method by which men of science establish the existence of that law is exactly the same as that by which we have established the trivial proposition about the sourness of hard and green apples. But we believe it in such an extensive, thorough, and unhesitating' manner because the universal experience of mankind verifies it, and we can verify it ourselves at any time; and that is the strongest possible foundation on which any natural law can rest.

So much, then, by way of proof that the method of establishing laws in science is exactly the same as that pursued in common life. Let us now turn to another matter (though really it is but another phase of the same question), and that is, the method by which, from the relations of certain phenomena, we prove that some stand in the position of causes towards the others.

I want to put the case clearly before you, and I will therefore show you what I mean by another familiar example. I will suppose that one of you, on coming down in the morning to the parlor of your house, finds that a tea-pot and some spoons which had been left in the room on the previous evening are gone, — the window is open, and you observe the mark of a dirty hand on the window-frame, and perhaps, in addition to that, you notice the impress of a hob-nailed shoe on the gravel outside. All these phenomena have struck your attention instantly, and before two seconds have passed you say, " Oh, somebody has broken open the window, entered the room, and run off with the spoons and the tea-pot!" That speech is out of your mouth in a moment. And you will probably add, "I know there has; I am quite sure of it!" You mean to say exactly what you know; but in reality you are giving expression to what is, in all essential particulars, an hypothesis. You do not *know* it at all; it is nothing but an hypothesis rapidly framed in your own mind. And it is an hypothesis founded on a long train of inductions and deductions.

What are those inductions and deductions, and how have you got at this hypothesis ? You have observed in the first place, that the window is open; but by a train of reasoning involving many inductions and deductions, you have probably arrived long before at the general law — and a very good one it is — that windows do not open of themselves; and you therefore conclude that something has opened the window. A second general law that you have arrived at in the same way is, that tea-pots and spoons do not go out of a window spontaneously, and you are satisfied that, as they are not now where you left them, they have been removed. In the third place, you look at the marks on the window-sill, and the shoe-marks outside, and you say that in all previous experience the former kind of mark has never been produced by anything else but the hand of a human being; and the same experience shows that no other animal but man at present wears shoes with hobnails in them such as would produce the marks in the gravel. I do not know, even if we could discover any of those "missing links" that are talked about, that they would help us to any other conclusion! At any rate the law which states our present experience is strong enough for my present purpose. You next reach the conclusion that, as these kind of marks have not been left by any other animal than man, or are liable to be formed in any other way than a man's hand and shoe, the marks in question have been formed by a man in that way. You have, further, a general law, founded on observation and experience, and that, too, is, I am sorry to say, a very universal and unimpeachable one, — that some men are thieves; and you assume at once from all these premisses — and that is what constitutes your hypothesis — that the man who made the marks outside and on the window-sill, opened the window, got into the room, and stole your tea-pot and spoons. You have now arrived at a *vera causa* ; — you have assumed a cause which, it is plain, is competent to produce all the phenomena you have observed. You can explain all these phenomena only by the hypothesis of a thief. But that is a hypothetical conclusion, of the justice of which you have no absolute proof at all; it is only rendered highly probable by a series of inductive and deductive reasonings.

I suppose your first action, assuming that you are a man of ordinary common sense, and that you have es-tablished this hypothesis to your own satisfaction, will very likely be to go off for the police, and set them on the track of the burglar, with the view to the recovery of your property. But just as you are starting with this object, some person comes in, and on learning what you are about, says, " My good friend, you are going on a great deal too fast. How do you know that the man who really made the marks took the spoons ? It might have been a monkey that took them, and the man may have merely looked in afterwards.,, You would probably reply, "Well, that is all very well, but you see it is contrary to all experience of the way tea-pots and spoons are abstracted; so that, at any rate, your hypothesis is less probable than mine.,, While you are talking the thing over in this way, another friend arrives, one of the good kind of people that I was talking of a little while ago. And he might say, " Oh, my dear sir, you are certainly going on a great deal too fast. You are most presumptuous. You admit that all these occurrences took place when you were fast asleep, at a time when you could not possibly have known anything about what was taking place. How do you know that the laws of Nature are not sus-pended during the night ? It may be that there has been some kind of supernatural interference in this case." In point of fact, he declares that your hypothesis is one of which you cannot at all demonstrate the truth, and that you are by no means sure that the laws of Nature are the same when you are asleep as when you are awake.

Well, now, you cannot at the moment answer that kind of reasoning. You feel that your worthy friend has you somewhat at a disadvantage. You will feel perfectly convinced in your own mind, however, that you are quite right, and you say to him, "My good friend, I can only be guided by the natural probabilities of the case, and if you will be kind enough to stand aside and permit me to pass, I will go and fetch the police." Well, we will suppose that your journey is successful, and that by good luck you meet with a policeman; that eventually the burglar is found with your property on his person, and the marks correspond to his hand and to his boots. Probably any jury would consider those facts a very good experimental verification of your hy-pothesis, touching the cause of the abnormal phenomena observed in your parlor, and would act accordingly.

Now, in this supposititious case, I have taken phe-nomena of a very common kind, in order that you might see what are the different steps in an ordinary process of reasoning, if you will only take the trouble to analyse it carefully. All the operations I have described, you will see, are involved in the mind of any man of sense in leading him to a conclusion as to the course he should take in order to make good a robbery and punish the offender. I say that you are led, in that case, to your conclusion by exactly the same train of reasoning as that which a man of science pursues when he is endeavouring to discover the origin and laws of the most occult phenomena. The process is, and always must be, the same; and precisely the same mode of reasoning was employed by Newton and Laplace in their endeavours to discover and define the causes of the movements of the heavenly bodies, as you, with your own common sense, would employ to detect a burglar. The only difference is, that the nature of the inquiry being more abstruse, every step has to be most carefully watched, so that there may not be a single crack or flaw in your hypothesis. A flaw or crack in many of the hypotheses of daily life may be of little or no moment as affecting the general correctness of the conclusions at which we may arrive; but, in a scientific inquiry, a fallacy, great or small, is always of importance, and is sure to be in the long run constantly productive of mischievous if not fatal results.

Do not allow yourselves to be misled by the common notion that an hypothesis is untrustworthy simply be-cause it is an hypothesis. It is often urged, in respect to some scientific conclusion, that, after all, it is only an hypothesis. But what more have we to guide us in nine-tenths of the most important affairs of daily life than hypotheses, and often very ill-based ones? So that in science, where the evidence of an hypothesis is subjected to the most rigid examination, we may rightly pursue the same course. You may have hypotheses, and hypotheses. A man may say, if he likes, that the moon is made of green cheese: that is an hypothesis.

But another man, who has devoted a great deal of time and attention to the subject, and availed himself of the most powerful telescopes and the results of the observa-tions of others, declares that in his opinion it is probably composed of materials very similar to those of which our own earth is made up: and that is also only an hypothesis. But I need not tell you that there is an enormous difference in the value of the two hypotheses. That one which is based on sound scientific knowledge is sure to have a corresponding value; and that which is a mere hasty random guess is likely to have but little value. Every great step in our progress in discovering causes has been made in exactly the same way as that which I have detailed to you. A person observing the occurrence of certain facts and phenomena asks, naturally enough, what process, what kind of operation known to occur in Nature applied to the particular case, will unravel and explain the mystery ? Hence you have the scientific hypothesis; and its value will be proportionate to the care and completeness with which its basis had been tested and verified. It is in these matters as in the commonest affairs of practical life: the guess of the fool will be folly, while the guess of the wise man will contain wisdom. In all cases, you see that the value of the result depends on the patience and faithfulness with which the investigator applies to his hypothesis every possible kind of verification.

ON THE PHYSICAL BASIS OF LIFE

IN order to make the title of this discourse generally intelligible, I have translated the term "Protoplasm," which is the scientific name of the substance of which I am about to speak, by the words " the physical basis of life." I suppose that, to many, the idea that there is such a thing as a physical basis, or matter, of life may be novel — so widely spread is the conception of life as a something which works through matter, but is independent of it; and even those .who are aware that matter and life are inseparably connected, may not be prepared for the conclusion plainly suggested by the phrase, " *the* physical basis or matter of life," that there is some one kind of matter who is common to all living beings, and that their endless diversities are bound together by a physical, as well as an ideal, unity. In fact, when first apprehended, such a doctrine as this appears almost shocking to common sense.

What, truly, can seem to be more obviously different from one another, in faculty, in form, and in substance, than the various kinds of living beings? What community of faculty can there be between the bright-coloured lichen, which so nearly resembles a mere mineral incrustation of the bare rock on which it grows, and the painter, to whom it is instinct with beauty, or the botanist, whom it feeds with knowledge ?

Again, think of the microscopic fungus — a mere infinitesimal ovoid particle, which finds space and du-ration enough to multiply into countless millions in the body of a living fly; and then of the wealth of foliage, the luxuriance of flower and fruit, which lies between this bald sketch of a plant and the giant pine of California, towering to the dimensions of a cathedral spire, or the Indian fig, which covers acres with its profound shadow, and endures while nations and empires come and go around its vast circumference. Or, turning to the other half of the world of life, picture to yourselves the great Finner whale, hugest of beasts that live, or have lived, disporting his eighty or ninety feet of bone, muscle and blubber, with easy roll, among waves in which the stoutest ship that ever left dockyard would flounder hopelessly; and contrast him with the invisible animalcules — mere gelatinous specks, multitudes of which could, in fact, dance upon the point of a needle with the same ease as the angels of the Schoolmen could, in imagination. With these images before your minds, you may well ask, what community of form, or structure, is there between the animalcule and the whale; or between the fungus and the fig-tree ? And, à fortiori, between all four ? Finally, if we regard substance, or material composition, what hidden bond can connect the flower which a girl wears in her hair and the blood which courses through her youthful veins; or, what is there in common between the dense and resisting mass of the oak, or the strong fabric of the tortoise, and those broad disks of glassy jelly which may be seen pulsating through the waters of a calm sea, but which drain away to mere films in the hand which raises them out of their element ?

Such objections as these must, I think, arise in the mind of every one who ponders, for the first time, upon the conception of a single physical basis of life underlying all the diversities of vital existence; but I propose to demonstrate to you that, notwithstanding these apparent difficulties, a threefold unity — namely, a unity of power or faculty, a unity of form, and a unity of substantial composition — does pervade the whole living world.

No very abstruse argumentation is needed, in the first place to prove that the powers, or faculties, of all kinds of living matter, diverse as they may be in degree, are substantially similar in kind.

Goethe has condensed a survey of all powers of man-kind into the well-known epigram: —

"Warum treibt sich das Volk so und schreit? Es will sich ernähren Kinder zeugen, und die nâhren so gut es vermag.

Weiter bringt es kein Mensch, stell' er sich wie er auch will."

In physiological language this means, that all the multifarious and complicated activities of man are comprehensible under three categories. Either they are immediately directed towards the maintenance and development of the body, or they effect transitory changes in the relative positions of parts of the body, or they tend towards the continuance of the species. Even those manifestations of intellect, of feeling, and of will, which we rightly name the higher faculties, are not excluded from this classification, inasmuch as to every one but the subject of them, they are known only as transitory changes in the relative positions of parts of the body. Speech, gesture, and every other form of human action are, in the long run, resolvable into muscular contraction, and muscular contraction is but a transitory change in the relative positions of the parts of a muscle. But the scheme which is large enough to embrace the activities of the highest form of life, covers all those of the lower creatures. The lowest plant, .or animalcule, feeds, grows, and reproduces its kind. In addition, all animals manifest those transitory changes of form which we class under irritability and contractility; and, it is more than probable, that when the vegetable world is thoroughly explored, we shall find all plants in possession of the same powers, at one time or other of their existence.

I am not now alluding to such phaenomena, at once rare and conspicuous, as those exhibited by the leaflets of the sensitive plants, or the stamens of the barberry, but to much more widely spread, and at the same time, more subtle and hidden, manifestations of vegetable contractility. You are doubtless aware that the common nettle owes its stinging property to the innumerable stiff and needle-like, though exquisitely delicate, hairs which cover its surface. Each stinging-needle tapers from a broad base to a slender summit, which, though rounded at the end, is of such microscopic fineness that it readily penetrates, and breaks off in, the skin. The whole hair consists of a very delicate outer case of wood, closely applied to the inner surface of which is a layer of semifluid matter, full of innumerable granules of extreme minuteness. This semi-fluid lining is protoplasm, which thus constitutes a kind of bag, full of a limpid liquid, and roughly corresponding in form with the interior of the hair which it fills. When viewed with a sufficiently high magnifying power, the protoplasmic layer of the nettle hair is seen to be in a condition of unceasing activity. Local contractions of the whole thickness of its substance pass slowly and gradually from point to point, and give rise to the appearance of progressive waves, just as the bending of successive stalks of corn by a breeze produces the apparent billows of a cornfield.

But, in addition to these movements, and independ-ently of them, the granules are driven, in relatively rapid streams, through channels in the protoplasm which seem to have a considerable amount of persistence. Most commonly, the currents in adjacent parts of the protoplasm take similar directions; and, thus, there is a general stream up one side of the hair and down the other. But this does not prevent the existence of partial currents which take different routes; and sometimes trains of granules may be seen coursing swiftly in opposite directions within a twenty-thousandth of an inch of one another; while, occasionally, opposite streams come into direct collision, and, after a longer or shorter struggle, one predominates. The cause of these currents seems to lie in contractions of the protoplasm which bounds the channels in which they flow, but which are so minute that the best microscopes show only their effects, and not themselves.

The spectacle afforded by the wonderful energies prisoned within the compass of the microscopic hair of a plant, which we commonly regard as a merely passive organism, is not easily forgotten by one who has watched its display, continued hour after hour, without pause or sign of weakening. The possible complexity of many other organic forms, seemingly as simple as the protoplasm of the nettle, dawns upon one; and the comparison of such a protoplasm to a body with an internal circulation, which has been put forward by an eminent physiologist, loses much of its startling character. Currents similar to those of the hairs of the nettle have been observed in a great multitude of very different plants, and weighty authorities have suggested that they probably occur, in more or less perfection, in all young vegetable cells. If such be the case, the wonderful noonday silence of a tropical forest is, after all, due only to the dulness of our hearing; and could our ears catch the murmur of these tiny Maelstroms, as they whirl in the innumerable myriads of living cells which constitute each tree, we should be stunned, as with the roar of a great city.

Among the lower plants, it is the rule rather than the exception, that contractility should be still more openly manifested at some periods of their existence. The protoplasm of Alga and Fungi becomes, under many circumstances, partially, or completely, freed from its woody case, and exhibits movements of its whole mass, or is propelled by the contractility of one, or more, hair-like prolongations of its body, which are called vibratile cilia. And, so far as the conditions of the manifesta-tion of the phaenomena of contractility have yet been studied, they are the same for the plant as for the animal. Heat and electric shocks influence both, and in the same way, though it may be in different degrees. It is by no means my intention to suggest that there is no difference in faculty between the lowest plant and the highest, or between plants and animals. But the difference between the powers of the lowest plant, or animal, and those of the highest, is one of degree, not of kind, and depends, as Milne-Edwards long ago so well pointed out, upon the extent to which the principle of the division of labour is carried out in the living economy. In the lowest organism all parts are competent to perform all functions, and one and the same portion of protoplasm may successfully take on the function of feeding, moving, or reproducing apparatus. In the highest, on the contrary, a great number of parts combine to perform each function, each part do-ing its allotted share of the work with great accuracy and efficiency, but being useless for any other purpose.

On the other hand, notwithstanding all the fundamental resemblances which exist between the powers of the protoplasm in plants and in animals, they present a striking difference (to which I shall advert more at length presently), in the fact that plants can manufacture fresh protoplasm out of mineral compounds, whereas animals are obliged to procure it ready made, and hence, in the long run, depend upon plants. Upon what condition this difference in the powers of the two great divisions of the world of life depends, nothing is at present known.

With such qualifications as arises out of the last-mentioned fact, it may be truly said that the acts of all living things are fundamentally one. Is any such unity predicable of their forms ? Let us seek in easily verified facts for a reply to this ques-tion. If a drop of blood be drawn by pricking one's finger, and viewed with proper precautions, and under a sufficiently high microscopic power, there will be seen, among the innumerable multitude of little, circular, discoidal bodies, or corpuscles, which float in it and give it its colour, a comparatively small number of colourless corpuscles, of somewhat larger size and very irregular shape. If the drop of blood be kept at the temperature of the body, these colourless corpuscles will be seen to exhibit a marvellous activity, changing their forms with great rapidity, drawing in and thrusting out prolongations of their substance, and creeping about as if they were independent organisms.

The substance which is thus active is a mass of pro-toplasm, and its activity differs in detail, rather than in principle, from that of the protoplasm of the nettle. Under sundry circumstances the corpuscle dies and becomes distended into a round mass, in the midst of which is seen a smaller spherical body, which existed, but was more or less hidden, in the living corpuscle, and is called its *nucleus*. Corpuscles of essentially similar structure are to be found in the skin, in the lining of the mouth, and scattered through the whole framework of the body. Nay, more; in the earliest condition of the human organism, in that state in which it has but just become distinguishable from the egg in which it arises, it is nothing but an aggregation of such corpuscles, and every organ of the body was, once, no more than such an aggregation.

Thus a nucleated mass of protoplasm turns out to be what may be termed the structural unit of the human body. As a matter of fact, the body, in its earliest state, is a mere multiple of such units; and in its perfect condition, it is a multiple of such units, variously modified.

But does the formula which expresses the essential structural character of the highest animal cover all the rest, as the statement of its powers and faculties covered that of all others ? Very nearly. Beast and fowl, reptile and fish, mollusk, worm, and polype, are all composed of structural units of the same character, namely, masses of protoplasm with a nucleus. There are sundry very low animals, each of which, structurally, is a mere colourless blood - corpuscle, leading an independent life. But, at the very bottom of the animal scale, even this simplicity becomes simplified, and all the phaenomena of life are manifested by a particle of prtoplasm without a nucleus. Nor are such organisms insignificant by reason of their want of complexity. It is a fair question whether the protoplasm of those simplest forms of life, which people an immense extent of the bottom of the sea, would not outweigh that of all the higher living beings which inhabit the land put together. And in ancient times, no less than at the present day, such living beings as these have been the greatest of rock builders.

What has been said of the animal world is no less true of plants. Imbedded in the protoplasm at the broad, or attached, end of the nettle hair, there lies a spheroidal nucleus. Careful examination further proves that the whole substance of the nettle is made up of a repetition of such masses of nucleated protoplasm, each con-tained in a wooden case, which is modified in form, sometimes into a woody fibre, sometimes into a duct or spiral vessel, sometimes into a pollen grain, or an ovule. Traced back to its earliest state, the nettle arises as the man does, in a particle of nucleated protoplasm. And in the lowest plants, as in the lowest animals, a single mass of such protoplasm may constitute the whole plant, or the protoplasm may exist without a nucleus.

Under these circumstances it may well be asked, how is one mass of non-nucleated protoplasm to be dis-tinguished from another? why call one "plant" and the other "animal"?

The only reply is that, so far as form is concerned, plants and animals are not separable, and that, in many cases, it is a mere matter of convention whether we call a given organism an animal or a plant. There is a living body called Æthalium septicum, *which appears upon decaying vegetable substances, and, in one of its forms, is common upon the surfaces of tan-pits. In this condition it is, to all intents and purposes, a fungus, and formerly was always regarded as such; but the remarkable investigations of De Bary have shown that, in another condition, the Æthulium is an actively loco-*motive creature, and takes in solid matters, upon which, apparently, it feeds, thus exhibiting the most characteristic feature of animality. Is this a plant; or is it an animal ? Is it both; or is it neither ? Some decide in favour of the last supposition, and establish an intermediate kingdom, a sort of biological No Man's Land for all these questionable forms. But, as it is admittedly impossible to draw any distinct boundary line between this no man's land and the vegetable world on the one hand, or the animal, on the other, it appears to me that this proceeding merely doubles the difficulty which, before, was single.

Protoplasm, simple or nucleated, is the formal basis of all life. It is the clay of the potter: which, bake it and paint it as he will, remains clay, separated by artifice, and not by nature, from the commonest brick or sun-dried clod.

Thus it becomes clear that all living powers are cog-nate, and that all living forms are fundamentally of one character. The researches of the chemist have revealed a no less striking uniformity of material composition in living matter. In perfect strictness, it is true that chemical investi-gation can tell us little or nothing, directly, of the com-position of living matter, inasmuch as such matter must needs die in the act of analysis, — and upon this very obvious ground, objections, which

I confess seem to me to be somewhat frivolous, have been raised to the drawing of any conclusions whatever respecting the composition of actually living matter, from that of the dead matter of life, which alone is accessible to us. But objectors of this class do not seem to reflect that it is also, in strictness, true that we know nothing about the composition of any body whatever, as it is. The state-ment that a crystal of calc-spar consists of carbonate of lime, is quite true, if we only mean that, by appropriate processes, it may be resolved into carbonic acid and quicklime. If you pass the same carbonic acid over the very quicklime thus obtained, you will obtain carbonate of lime again; but it will not be calc-spar, nor anything like it. Can it, therefore, be said that chemical analysis teaches nothing about the chemical composition of calc-spar ? Such a statement would be absurd; but it is hardly more so than the talk one occasionally hears about the uselessness of applying the results of chemical analysis to the living bodies which have yielded them.

One fact, at any rate, is out of reach of such refine-ments, and this is, that all the forms of protoplasm which have yet been examined contain the four elements, carbon, hydrogen, oxygen, and nitrogen, in very complex union, and that they be-have similarly towards several reagents. To this complex combination, the nature of which has never been determined with exactness, the name of Protein has been applied. And if we use this term with such caution as may properly arise out of our comparative ignorance of the things for which it stands, it may be truly said, that all protoplasm is proteinaceous, or, as the white, or albumen, of an egg is one of the commonest examples of a nearly pure proteine matter, we may say that all living matter is more or less albuminoid.

Perhaps it would not yet be safe to say that all forms of protoplasm are affected by the direct action of electric shocks; and yet the number of cases in which the contraction of protoplasm is shown to be affected by this agency increases every day.

Nor can it be affirmed with perfect confidence, that all forms of protoplasm are liable to undergo that peculiar coagulation at a temperature of 40° — 50° centigrade, which has been called "heat-stiffening," though Kühne's beautiful researches have proved this occurrence to take place in so many and such diverse living beings, that it is hardly rash to expect that the law holds good for all.

Enough has, perhaps, been said to prove the existence of a general uniformity in the character of the protoplasm, or physical basis, of life, in whatever group of living beings it may be studied. But it will be understood that this general uniformity by no means excludes any amount of special modifications of the fundamental substance. The mineral, carbonate of lime, assumes an immense diversity of characters, though no one doubts that, under all these Protean changes, it is one and the same thing.

And now, what is the ultimate fate, and what the origin, of the matter of life ?

Is it, as some of the older nattiralists supposed, dif-fused throughout the universe in molecules, which are indestructible and unchangeable in themselves; but, in endless transmigration, unite in innumerable permu-tations, into the diversified forms of life we know ? Or, is the matter of life composed of ordinary matter, differing from it only in the manner in which its atoms are aggregated ? Is it built up of ordinary matter, and again resolved into ordinary matter when its work is done ?

Modern science does not hesitate a moment between these alternatives. Physiology writes over the portals of life —

"Debemur morti nos nostraque,"

with a profounder meaning than the Roman poet at-tached to that melancholy line. Under whatever disguise it takes refuge, whether fungus or oak, worm or man, the living protoplasm not only ultimately dies and is resolved into its mineral and lifeless constituents, but is always dying, and, strange as the paradox may sound, could not live unless it died.

In the wonderful story of the *Peau de Chagrin*, the hero becomes possessed of a magical wild ass' skin, which yields him the means of gratifying all his wishes. But its surface represents the duration of the proprietor's life; and for every satisfied desire the skin shrinks in proportion to the intensity of fruition, until at length life and the last handbreadth of the *peau de chagrin*, disappear with the gratification of a last wish.

Balzac's studies had led him over a wide range of thought and speculation, and his shadowing forth of physiological truth in this strange story may have been intentional. At any rate, the matter of life is a veritable *peau de chagrin*, and for every vital act it is somewhat the smaller. All work implies waste, and the work of life results, directly or indirectly, in the waste of protoplasm.

Every word uttered by a speaker costs him some physical loss; and, in the strictest sense, he burns that others may have light — so much eloquence, so much of his body resolved into carbonic acid, water, and urea. It is clear that this process of expenditure cannot go on for ever. But, happily, the protoplasmic *peau de chagrin* differs from Balzac's in its capacity of being repaired, and brought back to its full size, after every exertion.

For example, this present lecture, whatever its intel-lectual worth to you, has a certain physical value to me, which is, conceivably, expressible by the. number of grains of protoplasm and other bodily substance wasted in maintaining my vital processes during its delivery. My *peau de chagrin* will be distinctly smaller at the end of the discourse than it was at the beginning. By and by, I shall probably have recourse to the substance commonly called mutton, for the purpose of stretching it back to its original size. Now this mutton was once the living protoplasm, more or less modified, of another animal — a sheep. As I shall eat it, it is the same matter altered, not only by death, but by exposure to sundry artificial operations in the process of cooking.

But these changes, whatever be their extent, have not rendered it incompetent to resume its old functions as matter of life. A singular inward laboratory, which I possess, will dissolve a certain portion of the modified protoplasm; the solution so formed will pass into my veins; and the subtle influences to which it will then be subjected will convert the dead protoplasm into living protoplasm, and transubstantiate sheep into man.

Nor is this all. If digestion were a thing to be trifled with, I might sup upon lobster, and the matter of life of the crustacean would undergo the same wonderful metamorphosis into humanity. And were I to return to my own place by sea, and undergo shipwreck, the crustacean might, and probably would, return the compliment, and demonstrate our common nature by turning my protoplasm into living lobster. Or, if nothing better were to be had, I might supply my wants with mere bread, and I should find the protoplasm of the wheat-plant to be convertible into man, with no more trouble than that of the sheep, and with far less, I fancy, than that of the lobster.

Hence it appears to be a matter of no great moment what animal, or what plant, I lay under contribution for protoplasm, and the fact speaks volumes for the general identity of that substance in all living beings. I share this catholicity of assimilation with other animals, all of which, so far as we know, could thrive equally well on the protoplasm of any of their fellows, or of any plant; but here the assimilative powers of the animal world cease. A solution of smelling-salts in water, with an infinitesimal proportion of some other saline matters, contains all the elementary bodies which enter into the composition of protoplasm; but, as I need hardly say, a hogshead of that fluid would not keep a hungry man from starving, nor would it save any animal whatever from a like fate. An animal can-not make protoplasm, but must take it ready-made from some other animal, or some plant — the animal's highest feat of constructive chemistry being to convert dead protoplasm into that living matter of life which is appropriate to itself.

Therefore, in seeking for the origin of protoplasm, we must eventually turn to the vegetable world. A fluid containing carbonic acid, water, and nitrogenous salts, which offers such a Barmecide feast to the animal, is a table richly spread to multitudes of plants; and, with a due supply of only such materials, many a plant will not only maintain itself in vigour, but grow and multiply until it has increased a million-fold, or a million million-fold, the quantity of protoplasm which it originally possessed; in this way building up the matter of life, to an indefinite extent, from the common matter of the universe.

Thus, the animal can only raise the complex substance of dead protoplasm to the higher power, as one may say, of living protoplasm; while the plant can raise the less complex substances — carbonic acid, water, and nitrogenous salts — to the same stage of living protoplasm, if not to the same level. But the plant also has its limitations. Some of the fungi, for example, appear to need higher compounds to start with; and no known plant can live upon the uncom-pounded elements of protoplasm. A plant supplied with pure carbon, hydrogen, oxygen, and nitrogen, phosphorus, sulphur, and the like, would as infallibly die as the animal in his bath of smelling-salts, though it would be surrounded by all the constituents of proto-plasm. Nor, indeed, need the process of simplification of vegetable food be carried so far as this, in order to arrive at the limit of the plant's thaumaturgy. Let water, carbonic acid, and all the other needful constituents be supplied except nitrogenous salts, and an ordinary plant will still be unable to manufacture protoplasm.

Thus the matter of life, so far as we know it (and we have no right to speculate on any other), breaks up, in consequence of that continual death which is the condition of its manifesting vitality, into carbonic acid, water, and nitrogenous compounds, which certainly possess no properties but those of ordinary matter. And out of these same forms of ordinary matter, and from none which are simpler, the vegetable world builds up all the protoplasm which keeps the animal world a-going. Plants are the accumulators of the power which animals distribute and disperse.

But it will be observed, that the existence of the matter of life depends on the pre-existence of certain com-pounds; namely, carbonic acid, water, and certain nitrogenous bodies. Withdraw any one of these three from the world, and all vital phaenomena come to an end. They are as necessary to the protoplasm of the plant, as the protoplasm of the plant is to that of the animal. Carbon, hydrogen, oxygen, and nitrogen are all lifeless bodies. Of these, carbon and oxygen unite in certain proportions and under certain conditions, to give rise to carbonic acid; hydrogen and oxygen produce water; nitrogen and other elements give rise to nitrogenous salts. These new compounds, like the elementary bodies of which they are composed, are lifeless. But when they are brought together, under certain conditions, they give rise to the still more complex body, protoplasm, and this protoplasm exhibits the phaenomena of life.

I see no break in this series of steps in molecular complication, and I am unable to understand why the language which is applicable to any one term of the series may not be used to any of the others. We think fit to call different kinds of matter carbon, oxygen, hydrogen, and nitrogen, and to speak of the various powers and activities of these substances as the properties of the matter of which they are composed.

When hydrogen and oxygen are mixed in a certain proportion, and an electric spark is passed through them, they disappear, and a quantity of water, equal in weight to the sum of their weights, appears in their place. There is not the slightest parity between the passive and active powers of the water and those of the oxygen and hydrogen which have given rise to it. At 32° Fahrenheit, and far below that temperature, oxygen and hydrogen are elastic gaseous bodies, whose particles tend to rush away from one another with great force. Water, at the same temperature, is a strong though brittle solid whose particles tend to cohere into definite geometrical shapes, and sometimes build up frosty imitations of the most complex forms of vegetable foil-age.

Nevertheless we call these, and many other strange phaenomena, the properties of the water, and we do not hesitate to believe that, in some way or another, they result from the properties of the component elements of the water. We do not assume that a something called "aquosity" entered into and took possession of the oxidated hydrogen as soon as it was formed, and then guided the aqueous particles to their places in the facets of the crystal, or amongst the leaflets of the hoar-frost. On the contrary, we live in the hope and in the faith that, by the advance of molecular physics, we shall by and by be able to see our way as clearly from the constituents of water to the properties of water, as we are now able to deduce the operations of a watch from the form of its parts and the manner in which they are put together.

Is the case in any way changed when carbonic acid, water, and nitrogenous salts disappear, and in their place, under the influence of pre-existing living protoplasm, an equivalent weight of the matter of life makes its appearance ?

It is true that there is no sort of parity between the properties of the components and the properties of the resultant, but neither was there in the case of the water. It is also true that what I have spoken of as the influence of pre-existing living matter is something quite unintelligible; but does anybody quite comprehend the *modus operandi* of an electric spark, which traverses a mixture of oxygen and hydrogen ?

What justification is there, then, for the assumption of the existence in the living matter of a something which has no representative, or correlative, in the not living matter which gave rise to it ? What better philosophical status has "vitality" than "aquosity"? And why should "vitality" hope for a better fate than the other "itys" which have disappeared since Martinus Scriblerus accounted for the operation of the meat-jack by its inherent "meat-roasting quality," and scorned the "materialism" of those who explained the turning of the spit by a certain mechanism worked by the draught of the chimney.

If scientific language is to possess a definite and con-stant signification whenever it is employed, it seems to me that we are logically bound to apply to the protoplasm, or physical basis of life, the same conceptions as those which are held to be legitimate elsewhere. If the phaenomena exhibited by water are its properties, so are those presented by protoplasm, living or dead, its properties.

If the properties of water may be properly said to result from the nature and disposition of its component molecules, I can find no intelligible ground for refusing to say that the properties of protoplasm result from the nature and disposition of its molecules.

But I bid you beware that, in accepting these con-clusions, you are placing your feet on the first rung of a ladder which, in most people's estimation, is the reverse of Jacob's, and leads to the antipodes of heaven. It may seem a small thing to admit that the dull vital actions of a fungus, or a foraminifer, are the properties of their protoplasm, and are the direct results of the nature of the matter of which they are composed. But if, as I have endeavoured to prove to you, their protoplasm is essentially identical with, and most readily converted into, that of any animal, I can discover no logical halting-place between the admission that such is the case, and the further concession that all vital action may, with equal propriety, be said to be the result of the molecular forces of the protoplasm which displays it. And if so, it must be true, in the same sense and to the same extent, that the thoughts to which I am now giving utterance, and your thoughts regarding them, are the expression of molecular changes in that matter of life which is the source of our other vital phænomena.

ON CORAL AND CORAL REEFS

THE marine productions which are commonly known by the names of "Corals" and "Corallines," were thought by the ancients to be sea-weeds, which had the singular property of becoming hard and solid, when they were fished up from their native depths and came into contact with the air.

" Sic et curalium, quo primum contigit auras Tempore durescit: mollis fuit herba sub undis,"

says Ovid (*Metam. XV*); and it was not until the seven-teenth century that Boccone was emboldened, by per-sonal experience of the facts, to declare that the holders of this belief were no better than "idiots," who had been misled by the softness of the outer coat of the living red coral to imagine that it was soft all through. Messer Boccone's strong epithet is probably undeserved, as the notion he controverts, in all likelihood, arose merely from the misinterpretation of the strictly true statement which any coral fisherman would make to a curious inquirer; namely, that the outside coat of the red coral is quite soft when it is taken out of the sea. At any rate, he did good service by eliminating this much error from the current notions about coral. But the belief that corals are plants remained, not only in the popular, but in the scientific mind; and it received what appeared to be a striking confirmation from the researches of Marsigli in 1706. For this naturalist, having the opportunity of observing freshly-taken red coral, saw that its branches were beset with what looked like delicate and beautiful flowers each having eight petals. It was true that these "flowers" could protrude and retract themselves, but their motions were hardly more extensive, or more varied, than those of the leaves of the sensitive plant; and therefore they could not be held to militate against the conclusion so strongly suggested by their form and their grouping upon the branches of a tree-like structure.

Twenty years later, a pupil of Marsigli, the young Marseilles physician, Peyssonel, conceived the desire to study these singular sea-plants, and was sent by the French Government on a mission to the Mediterranean for that purpose. The pupil undertook the investigation full of confidence in the ideas of his master, but being able to see and think for himself, he soon discovered that those ideas by no means altogether corresponded with reality. In an essay entitled "Traitè du Corail," which was communicated to the French Academy of Science, but which has never been published, Peyssonel writes: —

" Je fis fleurir le corail dans des vases pleins d'eau de mer, et j'observai que ce que nous croyons ètre la fleur de cette prètendue plante n'ètait au vrai, qu'un insecte semblable à une petite Ortie ou Poulpe. J'avais le plaisir de voir remuer les pattes, ou pieds, de cette Ortie, et ayant mis le vase plein d'eau où le corail ètait a une douce chaleur auprès du feu, tous les petits in-sectes s'èpanouirent. — L'Ortie sortie ètend les pieds, et forme ce que M. de Marsigli et moi avions pris pour les pètales de la fleur. Le calice de cette prètendue fleur est le corps meme de l'animal èavanc et sorti hors de la cellule."[2]

The comparison of the flowers of the coral to a "petite ortie," or "little nettle," is

---

2   This extract from Peyssonel's manuscript is given by M. Lacaze Duthiers in his valuable *Histoire Naturell du Corail* (1866).

perfectly just, but needs explanation. "Ortie de mer," or "sea-nettle," is, in fact, the French appellation for our " sea-anemone," a creature with which everybody, since the great aquarium mania, must have become familiar, even to the limits of boredom. In 1710, the great naturalist, Réaumur, had written a memoir for the express purpose of demonstrating that these "orties" are animals; and with .this important paper Peyssonel must necessarily have been familiar. Therefore, when he declared the "flowers" of the red coral to be little "orties," it was the same thing as saying that they were animals of the same general nature as sea-anemones. But to Peyssonel's contemporaries this was an extremely startling announcement. It was hard to imagine the existence of such a thing as an association of animals into a structure with stem and branches altogether like a plant, and fixed to the soil as a plant is fixed; and the naturalists of that day preferred not to imagine it. Even Réaumur could not bring himself to accept the notion, and France being blessed with Academicians, whose great function (as the late Bishop Wilson and an eminent modern writer have so well shown) is to cause sweetness and light to prevail, and to prevent such unmannerly fellows as Peyssonel from blurting out unedifying truths, they suppressed him; and, as aforesaid, his great work remained in manuscript, and may at this day be consulted by the curious in that state, in the Bibliothèque du Musèum d' Histoire Naturelle. Peyssonel, who evidently was a person of savage and untameable disposition, so far from appreciating the kindness of the Academicians in giving him time to reflect upon the unreasonableness, not to say rudeness, of making public statements in opposition to the views of some of the most distinguished of their body, seems bitterly to have resented the treatment he met with. For he sent all further communications to the Royal Society of London, which never had, and it is to be hoped never will have, anything of an academic con stitution; and finally he took himself off to Guadaloupe, and became lost to science altogether.

Fifteen or sixteen years after the date of Peyssonel's suppressed paper, the Abbe Trembley pubjished his wonderful researches upon the fresh-water Hydra Bernard de Jussieu and Guettard followed them up by like inquiries upon the marine sea-anemones and corallines ; Réaumur, convinced against his will of the entire justice of Peyssonel's views, adopted them, and made him a half-and-half apology in the preface to the next published volume of the " Mèmoires pour servir l'His-toire des Insectes;" and, from this time forth, Peyssonel's doctrine that corals are the work of animal organisms has been part of the body of established scientific truth.

Peyssonel, in the extract from his memoir already cited, compares the flower-like animal of the coral to a " poulpe," which is the French form of the name " polypus," — " the many - footed," — which the ancient naturalists gave to the soft-bodied cuttlefishes, which, like the coral animal, have eight arms, or tentacles, disposed around a central mouth. Réaumur, admitting the analogy indicated by Peyssonel, gave the name of *polypes,* not only to the sea-anemone, the coral animal, and the fresh-water Hydra, but to what are now known as the *Polyzoa,* and he termed the skeleton which they fabricate a *"polypier"* or "polypidom."

The progress of discovery, since Réaumur's time, has made us very completely acquainted with the structure and habits of all these polypes. We know that, among the sea-anemones and coral-forming animals, each poylpe has a mouth leading to a stomach, which is open at its inner end, and thus communicates freely with the general cavity of the body; that the tentacles placed round the mouth are hollow, and that they perform the part of arms in seizing and capturing prey. It is known that many of these creatures are capable of being multiplied by artificial division, the divided halves growing, after a time, into complete and separate animals; and that many are able to perform a very similar process naturally, in such a manner that one polype may, by repeated incomplete divisions, give rise to a sort of sheet, or turf, formed by innumerable connected, and yet independent, descendants. Or, what is still more common, a polype may throw out buds, which are converted into polypes, or branches bearing polypes, until a tree-like mass, sometimes of very considerable size, is formed.

This is what happens in the case of the red coral of commerce. A minute polype, fixed to the rocky bottom of the deep sea, grows up into a branched trunk. The end of every branch and twig is terminated by a polype; and all the polypes are connected together by a fleshy substance, traversed by innumerable canals which place each polype in communication with every other, and carry nourishment to the substance of the supporting stem. It is a sort of natural cooperative store, every polype helping the whole, at the same time as it helps itself. The interior of the stem, like that of the branches, is solidified by the deposition of carbonate of lime in its tissue, somewhat in the same fashion as our own bones are formed of animal matter impreg longer or a shorter time, according as its position affords more or less protection from the wear and tear of the waves.

The polypes which give rise to the white coral are found, as has been said, in the seas of all parts of the world; but in the temperate and cold oceans they are scattered and comparatively small in size, so that the skeletons of those which die do not accumulate in any considerable quantity. But it is otherwise in the greater part of the ocean which lies in the warmer parts of the world, comprised within a distance of about eighteen hundred miles on each side of the equator. Within the zone thus bounded, by far the greater part of the ocean is inhabited by coral polypes, which not only form very strong and large skeletons, but associate together into great masses, like the thickets and the meadow turf, or, better still, the accumulations of peat, to which plants give rise on dry land. These masses of stony matter, heaped up beneath the waters of the ocean, become as dangerous to mariners as so much ordinary rock, and to these, as to the common rock ridges, the seaman gives the name of " reefs."

Such coral reefs cover many thousand square miles in the Pacific and in the Indian Oceans. There is one reef, or rather great series of reefs, called the Barrier Reef, which stretches, almost continuously, for more than eleven hundred miles off the east coast of Australia. Multitudes of the islands in the Pacific are either reefs themselves, or are surrounded by reefs. The Red Sea is in many parts almost a maze of such reefs, and they abound no less in the West Indies, along the coast of Florida, and even as far north as the Bahama Islands. But it is a very remarkable circumstance that, within the area of what we may call the " coral zone," there are no coral reefs upon the west coast of America, nor upon the west coast of Africa; and it is a general fact that the reefs are interrupted, or absent, opposite the mouths of great rivers. The causes of this apparent caprice in the distribution of coral reefs are not far to seek. The polypes which fabricate them require for their vigorous growth a temperature which must not fall below 68° Fahrenheit all the year round, and this temperature is only to be found within the distance on each side of the equator which has been mentioned, or thereabouts. But even within the coral zone this degree of warmth is not everywhere to be had. On the west coast of America, and on the corresponding coast of Africa, the currents of cold water from the icy regions which surround the South Pole set northward, and it appears to be due to their cooling influence that the sea in these regions is free from the reef builders.

Again, the coral polypes cannot live in water which is rendered brackish by floods from the land, or which is perturbed by mud from the same source, and hence it is that they cease to exist opposite the mouths of rivers, which damage them in both these ways.

Such is the general distribution of the reef-building corals, but there are some very interesting and singular circumstances to be observed in the conformation of the reefs, when we consider them individually. The reefs, in fact, are of three different kinds; some of them stretch out from the shore, almost like a prolongation of the beach, covered only by shallow water, and in the case of an island, surrounding it like a fringe of no considerable breadth. These are termed "fringing reefs." Others are separated by a channel which may attain a width of many miles, and a depth of twenty or thirty fathoms or more, from the nearest land; and when this land is an island, the reef surrounds it like a low wall, and the sea between the reef and the land is, as it were, a moat inside this wall. Such reefs as these are called "encircling" when they surround an island; and " barrier" reefs, when they stretch parallel with the coast of a continent. In both these cases there is ordinary dry land inside the reef, and separated from it only by a narrower or a wider, a shallower or a deeper, space of sea,, which is called a "lagoon," or "inner passage." But there is a third kind of reef, of very common occurrence in the Pacific and Indian Oceans, which goes by the name of "atoll." This is, to all intents and purposes, an encircling reef, without anything to encircle; or, in other words, without an island in the middle of its lagoon. The atoll has exactly the appearance of a vast, irregularly oval, or circular, breakwater, enclosing smooth water in its midst. The depth of the water in the lagoon rarely exceeds twenty or thirty fathoms, but, outside the reef, it deepens with great rapidity to two hundred or three hundred fathoms. The depth immediately outside the barrier, or encircling, reefs, may also be very considerable; but, at the outer edge of a fringing reef, it does not amount usually to more than twenty or twenty-five fathoms; in other words, from one hundred and twenty to one hundred and fifty feet.

Thus, if the water of the ocean should be suddenly drained away, we should see the atolls rising from the sea-bed like vast truncated cones, and resembling so many volcanic craters, except that their sides would be steeper than those of an ordinary volcano. In the case of the encircling reefs, the cone, with the enclosed island, would look like Vesuvius with Monte Nuovo within the old crater of Somma; while, finally, the island with a fringing reef would have the appearance of an ordinary hill, or mountain, girded by a vast parapet, within which would lie a shallow moat. And the dry bed of the Pacific might afford grounds for an inhabitant of the moon to speculate upon the extraordinary subterranean activity to which these vast and numerous " craters " bore witness!

When the structure of a fringing reef is investigated, the bottom of the lagoon is found to be covered with fine whitish mud, which results from the breaking up of the dead corals. Upon this muddy floor there lie, here and there, growing corals, or occasionally great blocks of dead coral, which have been torn by storms from the outer edge of the reef, and washed into the lagoon. Shellfish and worms of various kinds abound; and fish, some of which prey upon the coral, sport in the deeper pools. But the corals which are to be seen growing in the shallow waters of the lagoon are of a different kind from those which abound on the outer edge of the reef, and of which the reef is built up. Close to the seaward edge of the reef, over which, even in calm weather, a surf almost always breaks, the coral rock is encrusted with a thick coat of a singular vegetable organism, which contains a great deal of lime — the so-called *Nullipora*. Beyond this, in the part of the edge of the reef which is always covered by the breaking waves, the living, true, reef-polypes make their appearance; and, in different forms, coat the. steep seaward face, of the reef to a depth of one hundred or even one hundred and fifty feet. Beyond this depth the sounding-lead rests, not upon the wall-like face of the reef, but on the ordinary shelving sea-bottom. And the distance to which a fringing reef extends from the land corresponds with that at which the sea has a depth of twenty or five-and-twenty fathoms.

If, as we have supposed, the sea could be suddenly withdrawn from around an island provided with a fringing reef, such as the Mauritius, the reef would present the aspect of a terrace, its seaward face, one hundred feet or more high, blooming with the animal flowers of the coral, while its surface would be hollowed out into a shallow and irregular moat-like excavation.

The coral mud, which occupies the bottom of the lagoon, and with which all the interstices of the coral skeletons which accumulate to form the reef are filled up, does not proceed from the washing action of the waves alone; innumerable fishes, and other creatures which prey upon the coral, add a very important contribution of finely-triturated calcareous matter; and the corals and mud becoming incorporated together, gradually harden and give rise to a sort of limestone rock, which may vary a good deal in texture. Sometimes it remains friable and chalky, but, more often, the infiltration of water, charged with carbonic acid, dissolves some of the calcareous matter, and deposits it elsewhere in the interstices of the nascent rock, thus glueing and cementing the particles together into a hard mass; or it may even dissolve the carbonate of lime more extensively, and re-deposit it in a crystalline form. On the beach of the lagoon, where the coral sand is washed into layers by the action of the waves, its grains become thus fused together into strata of a limestone, so hard that they ring when struck with a hammer, and inclined at a gentle angle, corresponding with that of the surface of the beach. The hard parts of the many animals which live upon the reef become imbedded in this coral limestone, so that a block may be full of shells of bivalves and univalves, or of sea-urchins; and even sometimes encloses the eggs of turtles in a state of petrification. The active and vigorous growth of the reef goes on only at the seaward margins, where the polypes are exposed to the wash of the surf, and are thereby provided with an abundant supply of air and of food. The interior portion of the reef may be regarded as almost wholly an accumulation of dead skeletons. Where a river comes down from the land there is a break in the reef, for the reasons which have been already mentioned.

The origin and mode of formation of a fringing reef, such as that just described, are plain enough. The embryos of the coral polypes have fixed themselves upon the submerged shore of the island, as far out as they could live, namely, to a depth of twenty or twenty-five fathoms. One generation has succeeded another, building itself up upon the dead skeletons of its predecessor. The mass has been consolidated by the infiltration of coral mud, and hardened by partial solution and redeposition, until a great rampart of coral rock one hundred or one hundred and fifty feet high on its seaward face has been formed all round the island, with only such gaps as result from the outflow of rivers, in the place of sally-ports.

The structure of the rocky accumulation in the en-circling reefs and in the atolls is essentially the same as in the fringing reef. But, in addition to the differences of depth inside and out, they present some other peculiarities. These reefs, and especially the atolls, are usually interrupted at one part of their circumference, and this part is always situated on the leeward side of the reef, or that which is the more sheltered side. Now, as all these reefs are situated within the region in which the tradewinds prevail, it follows that, on the north side of the equator, where the trade-wind is a northeasterly wind, the opening of the reef is on the southwest side: while in the southern hemisphere, where the trade-winds blow from the southeast, the opening lies to the northwest. The curious practical result follows from this structure, that the lagoons to these reefs really form admirable harbours, if a ship can only get inside them. But the main difference between the encircling reefs and the atolls, on the one hand, and the fringing reefs on the other, lies in the fact of the much greater depth of water on the seaward faces of the former. As a consequence of this fact, the whole of this face is not, as it is in the case of the fringing reef, covered with living coral polypes. For, as we have seen, these polypes cannot live at a greater depth than about twenty-five fathoms; and actual observation has shown that while, down to this depth, the sounding-lead will bring up branches of live coral from the outer wall of such a reef, at a greater depth it fetches to the surface nothing but dead coral and coral sand. We must, therefore, picture to ourselves an atoll, or an encircling reef, as fringed for one hundred feet, or more, from its summit, with coral polypes busily engaged in fabricating coral; while, below this comparatively narrow belt, its surface is a bare and smooth expanse of coral sand, supported upon and within a core of coral limestone. Thus, if the bed of the Pacific were suddenly laid bare, as was just now supposed, the appearance of the reef-mountains would be exactly the reverse of that presented by many high mountains on land. For these are white with snow at the top, while their bases are clothed with an abundant and gaudily-coloured vegetation. But the coral cones would look grey and barren below, while their summits would be gay with a richly-coloured parterre of flowerlike coral polypes.

The practical difficulties of sounding upon, and of bringing up portions of, the seaward face of an atoll or of an encircling reef, are so great, in consequence of the constant and dangerous swell which sets towards it, that no exact information concerning the depth to which the reefs are composed of coral has yet been obtained. There is no reason to doubt, however, that the reef-cone has the same structure from its summit to its base, and that its sea-wall is throughout mainly composed of dead coral.

And now arises a serious difficulty. If the coral polypes cannot live at a greater depth than one hundred or one hundred and fifty feet, how can they have built up the base of the reef-cone, which may be two thousand feet, or more, below the surface of the sea?

In order to get over this objection, it was at one time supposed that the reef-building polypes had settled upon the summits of a chain of submarine mountains. But what is there in physical geography to justify the assumption of the existence of a chain of mountains stretching for one thousand miles or more, and so nearly of the same height, that none should rise above the level of the sea, nor fall one hundred and fifty feet below that level?

How, again, on this hypothesis, are atolls to be ac-counted for, unless, as some have done, we take refuge in the wild supposition that every atoll corresponds with the crater of a submarine volcano? And what explanation does it afford of the fact that, in some parte of the ocean, only atolls and encircling reefs occur, while others present none but fringing reefs?

These and other puzzling facts remained insoluble until the publication, in the year 1840, of Mr. Darwin's famous work on coral reefs; in which a key was given to all the difficult problems connected with the subject, and every difficulty was shown to be capable of solution by deductive reasoning from a happy combination of certain well-established geological and biological truths. Mr. Darwin, in fact, showed that, so long as the level of the sea remains unaltered in any area in which coral reefs are being formed, or if the level of the sea relatively to that of the land is falling, the only reefs which can be formed are fringing reefs. While if, on the contrary, the level of the sea is rising relatively to that of the land, at a rate not faster than that at which the upward growth of the coral can keep pace with it, the reef will gradually pass from the condition of a fringing, into that of an encircling or barrier reef. And, finally, that if the relative level of the sea rise so much that the encircled land is completely submerged, the reef must necessarily pass into the condition of an atoll.

For, suppose the relative level of the sea to remain stationary, after a fringing reef has reached that distance from the land at which the depth of water amounts to one hundred and fifty feet. Then the reef cannot extend seaward by the migration of coral germs, because these coral germs would find the bottom of the sea to be too deep for them to live in. And the only manner in which the reef could extend outwards, would be by the gradual accumulation, at the foot of its seaward face, of a talus of coral fragments torn off by the violence of the waves, which talus might, in course of time, become high enough to bring its upper surface within the limits of coral growth, and in that manner provide a sort of factitious sea-bottom upon which the coral embryos might perch. If, on the other hand, the level of the sea were slowly and gradually lowered, it is clear that the parts of its bottom originally beyond the limit of coral growth would gradually be brought within the required distance of the surface, and thus the reef might be indefinitely extended. But this process would give rise neither to an encircling reef nor to an atoll, but to a broad belt of upheaved coral rock, increasing the dimensions of the dry land, and continuous seawards with the fresh fringing reef.

Suppose, however, that the sea-level rose instead of falling, at the same slow and gradual rate at which we know it to be rising in some parts of the world, — not more, in fact, than a few inches, or, at most, a foot or two, in a hundred years. Then, while the reef would be unable to extend itself seaward, the sea-bottom outside it being gradually more and more removed from the depth at which the life of the coral polypes is possible, it would be able to grow upwards as fast as the sea rose. But the growth would take place almost exclusively around the circumference of the reef, this being the only region in which the coral polypes would find the conditions favourable for their existence. The bottom of the lagoon would be raised, in the main, only by the coral débris and coral mud, formed in the manner already described; consequently, the margins of the reef would rise faster than the bottom, or, in other words, the lagoon would constantly become deeper. And, at the same time, it would, gradually increase in breadth; as the rising sea, covering more of the land, would occupy a wider space between the edge of the reef and what remained of the land. Thus the rising sea would eventually convert a large island with a fringing reef into a small island surrounded by an encircling reef. And it will be obvious that when the rising of the sea has gone so far as completely to cover the highest points of the island, the reef will have passed into the condition of an atoll.

But how is it possible that the relative level of the land and sea should be altered to this extent ? Clearly, only in one of two ways: either the sea must have risen over those areas which are now covered by atolls and encircling reefs; or, the land upon which the sea rests must have been depressed to a corresponding extent.

If the sea has risen, its rise must have taken place over the whole world simultaneously, and it must have risen to the same height over all parts of the coral zone. Grounds have been shown for the belief that the general level of the sea may have been different at different times; it has been suggested, for example, that the accumulation of ice about the poles during one of the cold periods of the earth's history necessarily implies a diminution in the volume of the sea proportioned to the amount of its water thus permanently locked up in the Arctic and Antarctic ice-cellars; while, in the warm periods, the greater or less disappearance of the polar ice-cap implies a corresponding addition of water to the ocean. And no doubt this reasoning must be admitted to be sound in principle; though it is very hard to say what practical effect the additions and subtractions thus made have had on the level of the ocean; inasmuch as such additions and subtractions might be either intensified or. nullified, by contemporaneous changes in the level of the land. And no one has yet shown that any such great melting of polar ice, and consequent raising of the level of the water of the ocean, has taken place since the existing atolls began to be formed.

In the absence of any evidence that the sea has ever risen to the extent required to give rise to the encircling reefs and the atolls, Mr. Darwin adopted the opposite hypothesis, viz., that the land has undergone extensive and slow depression in those localities in which these structures exist.

It seems, at first, a startling paradox, to suppose that the land is less fixed than the sea; but that such is the case is the uniform testimony of geology. Beds of sandstone or limestone, thousands of feet thick, and all full of marine remains, occur in various parts of the earth's surface, and prove, beyond a doubt, that when these beds were formed, that portion of the sea-bottom which they then occupied underwent a slow and gradual depression to a distance which cannot have been less than the thickness of those beds, and may have been very much greater. In supposing, therefore, that the great areas of the Pacific and of the Indian Ocean, over which atolls and encircling reefs are found scattered, have undergone a depression of some hundreds, or, it may be, thousands of feet, Mr. Darwin made a supposition which had nothing forced or improbable, but was entirely in accordance with what we know to have taken place over similarly extensive areas, in other periods of the world's history. But Mr. Darwin sub-jected his hypothesis to an ingenious indirect test. If his view be correct, it is clear that neither atolls, nor encircling reefs, should be found in those portions of the ocean in which we have reason to believe, on independent grounds, that the sea-bottom has long been either stationary, or slowly rising. Now it is known that, as a general rule, the level of the land is either stationary, or is undergoing a slow upheaval, in the neighborhood of active volcanoes; and, therefore, neither atolls nor encircling reefs ought to be found in regions in which volcanoes are numerous and active. And this turns out to be the case. Appended to Mr. Darwin's great work on coral reefs, there is a map on which atolls and encircling reefs are indicated by one colour, fringing reefs by another, and active volcanoes by a third. And it is at once obvious that the lines of active volcanoes lie around the margins of the areas occupied by the atolls and the encircling reefs. It is exactly as if the upheaving volcanic agencies had lifted up the edges of these great areas, while their centres had undergone a corresponding depression. An atoll area may, in short, be pictured as a kind of basin, the margins of which have been pushed up by the subterranean forces, to which the craters of the volcanoes have, at intervals, given vent.

Thus we must imagine the area of the Pacific now covered by the Polynesian Archipelago, as having been, at some former time, occupied by large islands, or, may be, by a great continent, with the ordinarily diversified surface of plain, and hill, and mountain chain. The shores of this great land were doubtless fringed by coral reefs; and, as it slowly underwent depression, the hilly regions, converted into islands, became, at first, surrounded by fringing reefs, and then, as depression went on, these became converted into encircling reefs, and these, finally, into atolls, until a maze of reefs and coral-girdled islets took the place of the original land masses.

Thus the atolls and the encircling reefs furnish us with clear, though indirect, evidence of changes in the physical geography of large parts of the earth's surface; and even, as my lamented friend, the late Professor Jukes, has suggested, give us indications of the manner: in which some of the most puzzling facts connected with the distribution of animals have been brought about. For example, Australia and New Guinea are separated by Torres Straits, a broad belt of sea one hundred or one hundred and twenty miles wide. Nevertheless, there is in many respects a curious resemblance between the land animals which inhabit New Guinea and the land animals which inhabit Australia. But, at the same time, the marine shellfish which are found in the shallow waters of the shores of New Guinea are quite different from those which are met with upon the coasts of Australia. Now, the eastern end of Torres Straits is full of atolls, which, in fact, form the northern termination of the Great Barrier Reef which skirts the eastern coast of Australia. It follows, therefore, that the eastern end of Torres Straits is an area of depression, and it is very possible, and on many grounds highly probable, that, in former times, Australia and New Guinea were directly connected together, and that Torres Straits did not exist. If this were the case, the existence of cassowaries and of marsupial quadrupeds, both in New Guinea and in Australia, becomes intelligible; while the difference between the littoral molluscs of the north and.the south shores of Torres Straits is readily explained by the great probability that, when the depression in question took place, and what was, at first, an arm of the sea became converted into a strait separating Australia from New Guinea, the northern shore of this new sea became tenanted with marine animals from the north, while the southern shore was peopled by immigrants from the already existing marine Australian fauna. Inasmuch as the growth of the reef depends upon that of successive generations of coral polypes, and as each generation takes a certain time to grow to its full size, and can only separate its calcareous skeleton from the water in which it lives at a certain rate, it is clear that the reefs are records not only of changes in physical geography, but of the lapse of time. It is by no means easy, however, to estimate the exact value of reef-chronology, and the attempts which have been made to determine the rate at which a reef grows vertically have yielded anything but precise results. A cautious writer, Mr. Dana, whose extensive study of corals and coral reefs makes him an eminently competent judge, states his conclusion in the following terms: —

" The rate of growth of the common branching madrepore is not over one and a half inches a year. As the branches are open, this would not be equivalent to more than half an inch in height of solid coral for the whole surface covered by the madrepore; and, as they are also porous, to not over three-eighths of an inch of solid limestone. But a coral plantation has large bare patches without corals, and the coral sands are widely distributed by currents, part of them to depths over one hundred feet where there are no living corals; not more than one-sixth of the surface of a reef region is, in fact, covered with growing species. This reduces the three-eighths to *one-sixteenth*. Shells and other organic relics may contribute one-fourth as much as corals. At the outside, the average upward increase of the whole reef-ground per year would not exceed *one-eighth* of an inch.

" Now some reefs are at least two thousand feet thick, which at one-eighth of an inch a year, corresponds to one hundred and ninety-two thousand years."[3]

Halve, or quarter, this estimate if you will, in order to be certain of erring upon the right side, and still there remains a prodigious period during which the ancestors of existing coral polypes have been undis-turbedly at work; and during which, therefore, the climatal conditions over the coral area must have been much what they are now.

And all this lapse of time has occurred within the most recent period of the history of the earth. The remains of reefs formed by coral polypes of different kinds from those which exist now, enter largely into the composition of the limestones of the Jurassic period; and still more widely different coral polypes have contributed their quota to the vast thickness of the carboniferous and Devonian strata. Then as regards the latter group of rocks in America, the high authority already quoted tells us: —

"The Upper Helderberg period is eminently the coral reef period of the palaeozoic ages. Many of the rocks abound in coral, and are as truly coral reefs as the modern reefs of the Pacific. The corals are some-times standing on the rocks in the position they had when growing: others are lying in fragments, as they were broken and heaped by the waves; and others were reduced to a compact limestone by the finer trituration before consolidation into rock. This compact variety is the most common kind among the coral reef rocks of the present seas; and it often contains but few distinct fossils, although formed in water that abounded in life. At the fall of the Ohio, near Louisville, there is a magnificent display of the old reef. Hemispherical *Favorites*, five or six feet in diameter, lie there nearly. as perfect as when they were covered by their flower-like polypes; and besides these, there are various branching corals, and a profusion of *Cyathophyllia*, or cup-corals." [4]

Thus, in all the great periods of the earth's history of which we know anything,

---

3   Dana, Manual of Geology, p. 591.

4   Dana, Manual of Geology, p. 272.

a part of the then living matter has had the form of polypes, competent to separate from the water of the sea the carbonate of lime necessary for their own skeletons. Grain by grain, and particle by particle, they have built up vast masses of rock, the thickness of which is measured by hundreds of feet, and their area by thousands of square miles. The slow oscillations of the crust of the earth, producing great changes in the distribution of land and water, have often obliged the living matter of the coral-builders to shift the locality of its operations; and, by variation and adaptation to these modifications of condition, its forms have as often changed. The work it has done in the past is, for the most part, swept away, but fragments remain, and, if there were no other evidence, suffice to prove the general constancy of the operations of Nature in this world, through periods of almost inconceivable duration.

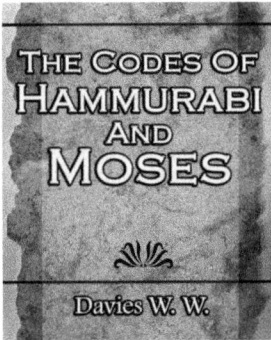

The Codes Of Hammurabi And Moses
W. W. Davies

QTY

The discovery of the Hammurabi Code is one of the greatest achievements of archaeology, and is of paramount interest, not only to the student of the Bible, but also to all those interested in ancient history...

Religion   ISBN: *1-59462-338-4*   **Pages:132**
MSRP $12.95

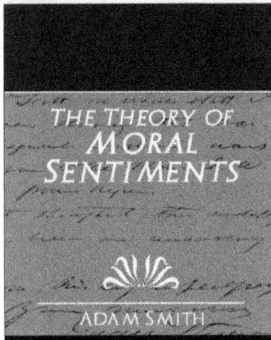

The Theory of Moral Sentiments
Adam Smith

QTY

This work from 1749. contains original theories of conscience amd moral judgment and it is the foundation for systemof morals.

Philosophy ISBN: *1-59462-777-0*   **Pages:536**
MSRP $19.95

Jessica's First Prayer
Hesba Stretton

QTY

In a screened and secluded corner of one of the many railway-bridges which span the streets of London there could be seen a few years ago, from five o'clock every morning until half past eight, a tidily set-out coffee-stall, consisting of a trestle and board, upon which stood two large tin cans, with a small fire of charcoal burning under each so as to keep the coffee boiling during the early hours of the morning when the work-people were thronging into the city on their way to their daily toil...

Childrens   ISBN: *1-59462-373-2*   **Pages:84**
MSRP $9.95

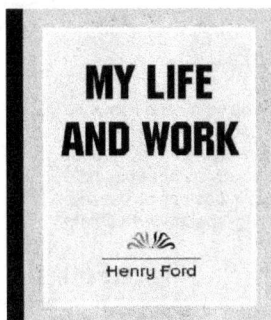

My Life and Work
Henry Ford

QTY

Henry Ford revolutionized the world with his implementation of mass production for the Model T automobile. Gain valuable business insight into his life and work with his own auto-biography... "We have only started on our development of our country we have not as yet, with all our talk of wonderful progress, done more than scratch the surface. The progress has been wonderful enough but..."

Biographies/   ISBN: *1-59462-198-5*   **Pages:300**
MSRP $21.95

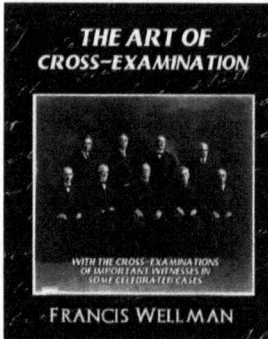

The Art of Cross-Examination
Francis Wellman

QTY

I presume it is the experience of every author, after his first book is published upon an important subject, to be almost overwhelmed with a wealth of ideas and illustrations which could readily have been included in his book, and which to his own mind, at least, seem to make a second edition inevitable. Such certainly was the case with me; and when the first edition had reached its sixth impression in five months, I rejoiced to learn that it seemed to my publishers that the book had met with a sufficiently favorable reception to justify a second and considerably enlarged edition. ..

Pages:412

Reference   ISBN: *1-59462-647-2*   *MSRP $19.95*

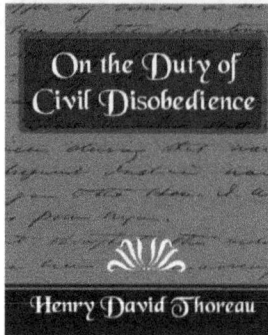

On the Duty of Civil Disobedience
Henry David Thoreau

QTY

Thoreau wrote his famous essay, On the Duty of Civil Disobedience, as a protest against an unjust but popular war and the immoral but popular institution of slave-owning. He did more than write—he declined to pay his taxes, and was hauled off to gaol in consequence. Who can say how much this refusal of his hastened the end of the war and of slavery ?

Law   ISBN: *1-59462-747-9*   **Pages:48**

MSRP $7.45

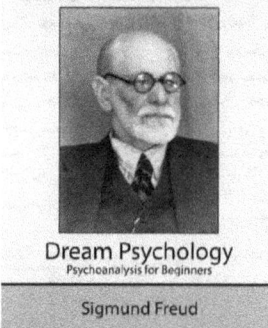

Dream Psychology Psychoanalysis for Beginners
Sigmund Freud

QTY

Sigmund Freud, born Sigismund Schlomo Freud (May 6, 1856 - September 23, 1939), was a Jewish-Austrian neurologist and psychiatrist who co-founded the psychoanalytic school of psychology. Freud is best known for his theories of the unconscious mind, especially involving the mechanism of repression; his redefinition of sexual desire as mobile and directed towards a wide variety of objects; and his therapeutic techniques, especially his understanding of transference in the therapeutic relationship and the presumed value of dreams as sources of insight into unconscious desires.

Pages:196

Psychology   ISBN: *1-59462-905-6*   *MSRP $15.45*

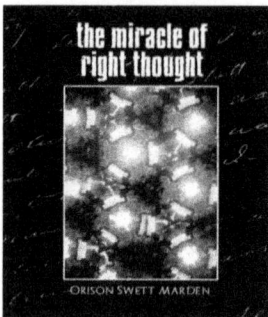

The Miracle of Right Thought
Orison Swett Marden

QTY

Believe with all of your heart that you will do what you were made to do. When the mind has once formed the habit of holding cheerful, happy, prosperous pictures, it will not be easy to form the opposite habit. It does not matter how improbable or how far away this realization may see, or how dark the prospects may be, if we visualize them as best we can, as vividly as possible, hold tenaciously to them and vigorously struggle to attain them, they will gradually become actualized, realized in the life. But a desire, a longing without endeavor, a yearning abandoned or held indifferently will vanish without realization.

Pages:360

Self Help   ISBN: *1-59462-644-8*   *MSRP $25.45*

The Rosicrucian Cosmo-Conception Mystic Christianity *by Max Heindel*   ISBN: 1-59462-188-8   **$38.95**
The Rosicrucian Cosmo-conception is not dogmatic, neither does it appeal to any other authority than the reason of the student. It is: not controversial, but is: sent forth in the, hope that it may help to clear...   New Age/Religion Pages 646

Abandonment To Divine Providence *by Jean-Pierre de Caussade*   ISBN: 1-59462-228-0   **$25.95**
"The Rev. Jean Pierre de Caussade was one of the most remarkable spiritual writers of the Society of Jesus in France in the 18th Century. His death took place at Toulouse in 1751. His works have gone through many editions and have been republished...   Inspirational/Religion Pages 400

Mental Chemistry *by Charles Haanel*   ISBN: 1-59462-192-6   **$23.95**
Mental Chemistry allows the change of material conditions by combining and appropriately utilizing the power of the mind. Much like applied chemistry creates something new and unique out of careful combinations of chemicals the mastery of mental chemistry...   New Age Pages 354

The Letters of Robert Browning and Elizabeth Barret Barrett 1845-1846 vol II   ISBN: 1-59462-193-4   **$35.95**
by Robert Browning and Elizabeth Barrett   Biographies Pages 596

Gleanings In Genesis (volume I) *by Arthur W. Pink*   ISBN: 1-59462-130-6   **$27.45**
Appropriately has Genesis been termed "the seed plot of the Bible" for in it we have, in germ form, almost all of the great doctrines which are afterwards fully developed in the books of Scripture which follow...   Religion/Inspirational Pages 420

The Master Key *by L. W. de Laurence*   ISBN: 1-59462-001-6   **$30.95**
In no branch of human knowledge has there been a more lively increase of the spirit of research during the past few years than in the study of Psychology, Concentration and Mental Discipline. The requests for authentic lessons in Thought Control, Mental Discipline and...   New Age/Business Pages 422

The Lesser Key Of Solomon Goetia *by L. W. de Laurence*   ISBN: 1-59462-092-X   **$9.95**
This translation of the first book of the "Lernegton" which is now for the first time made accessible to students of Talismanic Magic was done, after careful collation and edition, from numerous Ancient Manuscripts in Hebrew, Latin, and French...   New Age/Occult Pages 92

Rubaiyat Of Omar Khayyam *by Edward Fitzgerald*   ISBN: 1-59462-332-5   **$13.95**
Edward Fitzgerald, whom the world has already learned, in spite of his own efforts to remain within the shadow of anonymity, to look upon as one of the rarest poets of the century, was born at Bredfield, in Suffolk, on the 31st of March, 1809. He was the third son of John Purcell...   Music Pages 172

Ancient Law *by Henry Maine*   ISBN: 1-59462-128-4   **$29.95**
The chief object of the following pages is to indicate some of the earliest ideas of mankind, as they are reflected in Ancient Law, and to point out the relation of those ideas to modern thought.   Religiom/History Pages 452

Far-Away Stories *by William J. Locke*   ISBN: 1-59462-129-2   **$19.45**
"Good wine needs no bush, but a collection of mixed vintages does. And this book is just such a collection. Some of the stories I do not want to remain buried for ever in the museum files of dead magazine-numbers an author's not unpardonable vanity..."   Fiction Pages 272

Life of David Crockett *by David Crockett*   ISBN: 1-59462-250-7   **$27.45**
"Colonel David Crockett was one of the most remarkable men of the times in which he lived. Born in humble life, but gifted with a strong will, an indomitable courage, and unremitting perseverance...   Biographies/New Age Pages 424

Lip-Reading *by Edward Nitchie*   ISBN: 1-59462-206-X   **$25.95**
Edward B. Nitchie, founder of the New York School for the Hard of Hearing, now the Nitchie School of Lip-Reading, Inc, wrote "LIP-READING Principles and Practice". The development and perfecting of this meritorious work on lip-reading was an undertaking...   How-to Pages 400

A Handbook of Suggestive Therapeutics, Applied Hypnotism, Psychic Science   ISBN: 1-59462-214-0   **$24.95**
by Henry Munro   Health/New Age/Health/Self-help Pages 376

A Doll's House: and Two Other Plays *by Henrik Ibsen*   ISBN: 1-59462-112-8   **$19.95**
Henrik Ibsen created this classic when in revolutionary 1848 Rome. Introducing some striking concepts in playwriting for the realist genre, this play has been studied the world over.   Fiction/Classics/Plays 308

The Light of Asia *by sir Edwin Arnold*   ISBN: 1-59462-204-3   **$13.95**
In this poetic masterpiece, Edwin Arnold describes the life and teachings of Buddha. The man who was to become known as Buddha to the world was born as Prince Gautama of India but he rejected the worldly riches and abandoned the reigns of power when...   Religion/History/Biographies Pages 170

The Complete Works of Guy de Maupassant *by Guy de Maupassant*   ISBN: 1-59462-157-8   **$16.95**
"For days and days, nights and nights, I had dreamed of that first kiss which was to consecrate our engagement, and I knew not on what spot I should put my lips..."   Fiction/Classics Pages 240

The Art of Cross-Examination *by Francis L. Wellman*   ISBN: 1-59462-309-0   **$26.95**
Written by a renowned trial lawyer, Wellman imparts his experience and uses case studies to explain how to use psychology to extract desired information through questioning.   How-to/Science/Reference Pages 408

Answered or Unanswered? *by Louisa Vaughan*   ISBN: 1-59462-248-5   **$10.95**
Miracles of Faith in China   Religion Pages 112

The Edinburgh Lectures on Mental Science (1909) *by Thomas*   ISBN: 1-59462-008-3   **$11.95**
This book contains the substance of a course of lectures recently given by the writer in the Queen Street Hall, Edinburgh. Its purpose is to indicate the Natural Principles governing the relation between Mental Action and Material Conditions...   New Age/Psychology Pages 148

Ayesha *by H. Rider Haggard*   ISBN: 1-59462-301-3   **$24.95**
Verily and indeed it is the unexpected that happens! Probably if there was one person upon the earth from whom the Editor of this, and of a certain previous history, did not expect to hear again...   Classics Pages 380

Ayala's Angel *by Anthony Trollope*   ISBN: 1-59462-352-X   **$29.95**
The two girls were both pretty, but Lucy who was twenty-one who supposed to be simple and comparatively unattractive, whereas Ayala was credited, as her Bombwhat romantic name might show, with poetic charm and a taste for romance. Ayala when her father died was nineteen...   Fiction Pages 484

The American Commonwealth *by James Bryce*   ISBN: 1-59462-286-8   **$34.45**
An interpretation of American democratic political theory. It examines political mechanics and society from the perspective of Scotsman James Bryce   Politics Pages 572

Stories of the Pilgrims *by Margaret P. Pumphrey*   ISBN: 1-59462-116-0   **$17.95**
This book explores pilgrims religious oppression in England as well as their escape to Holland and eventual crossing to America on the Mayflower, and their early days in New England...   History Pages 268

QTY

The Fasting Cure *by Sinclair Upton*   ISBN: *1-59462-222-1*   **$13.95**

In the Cosmopolitan Magazine for May, 1910, and in the Contemporary Review (London) for April, 1910, I published an article dealing with my experiences in fasting. I have written a great many magazine articles, but never one which attracted so much attention...   New Age/Self Help/Health Pages 164

Hebrew Astrology *by Sepharial*   ISBN: *1-59462-308-2*   **$13.45**

In these days of advanced thinking it is a matter of common observation that we have left many of the old landmarks behind and that we are now pressing forward to greater heights and to a wider horizon than that which represented the mind-content of our progenitors...   Astrology Pages 144

Thought Vibration or The Law of Attraction in the Thought World   ISBN: *1-59462-127-6*   **$12.95**

by William Walker Atkinson   *Psychology/Religion Pages 144*

Optimism *by Helen Keller*   ISBN: *1-59462-108-X*   **$15.95**

Helen Keller was blind, deaf, and mute since 19 months old, yet famously learned how to overcome these handicaps, communicate with the world, and spread her lectures promoting optimism. An inspiring read for everyone...   Biographies/Inspirational Pages 84

Sara Crewe *by Frances Burnett*   ISBN: *1-59462-360-0*   **$9.45**

In the first place, Miss Minchin lived in London. Her home was a large, dull, tall one, in a large, dull square, where all the houses were alike, and all the sparrows were alike, and where all the door-knockers made the same heavy sound...   Childrens/Classic Pages 88

The Autobiography of Benjamin Franklin *by Benjamin Franklin*   ISBN: *1-59462-135-7*   **$24.95**

The Autobiography of Benjamin Franklin has probably been more extensively read than any other American historical work, and no other book of its kind has had such ups and downs of fortune. Franklin lived for many years in England, where he was agent...   Biographies/History Pages 332

Name	
Email	
Telephone	
Address	
City, State ZIP	

☐ **Credit Card**   ☐ **Check / Money Order**

Credit Card Number	
Expiration Date	
Signature	

Please Mail to: Book Jungle
PO Box 2226
Champaign, IL 61825
or Fax to: 630-214-0564

ORDERING INFORMATION

web*: www.bookjungle.com*
email*: sales@bookjungle.com*
fax*: 630-214-0564*
mail*: Book Jungle PO Box 2226 Champaign, IL 61825*
or PayPal *to sales@bookjungle.com*

Please contact us for bulk discounts

DIRECT-ORDER TERMS

**20% Discount if You Order
Two or More Books**
Free Domestic Shipping!
Accepted: Master Card, Visa,
Discover, American Express